JUST FOLLOW

Best Life Ever: *Following God*

40 Day Global Prayer Journey

JUST FOLLOW

Best Life Ever: *Following God*

40 Day Global Prayer Journey

CRAIG CARTER

Edition: 1.72 – First printing January 2025
Publisher: Courageous Third LLC
www.ReadCraigCarter.com

Bible scripture quotations are taken from various translations.
All rights to these translations are retained by their original publishers.

Cover Design: Gracie Miraglia — *footsteps of heaven, walking with God*

JUST FOLLOW: UNLOCK THE BEST LIFE EVER

Are you FULLY ALIVE?
Do you crave an extraordinary life?
You can — by letting go of control and just following God.

Do you like to feel in control? I used to.
Embark with a Corporate Finance Controller and Project Manager on a transformative 40-day journey through South Korea, China, and the USA. Discover how following God leads to unparalleled joy, incredible adventure, radical deep love, constant prayer, and at times — profound pain.

Most hesitate in fear to embrace this path of following — courage is essential. God is inviting you to experience the Best Life Ever.

The choice is yours.
Will you Just Follow?

DEDICATION

To my Lord Jesus and dearest friend — on this 40-day
journey You revealed how the Great Path, this best life
ever, is simply walking with you, just following.
Thank you for this Best Life Ever.

To Cristina, my sweet tender wife —
who is the air I breath, invisible to others.
You are my greatest gift from God,
My Ruby.
The travels and this path have been challenging.
I appreciate you and thank you for giving me the
freedom to follow God and to
bless many people from many nations.

To Benjamin our son —
who walks with God, deeply caring, loyal and
praying, hands clasped with mine to journey.

To Joshua our son —
wise counselor with God's wisdom, tuned to the
hearts of others, observant, steady tank-like power.

To Cesar —
my beloved father-in-law who is already in heaven.
I respect you and thank you,
as you are the role-model for how to lovingly raise a
beautiful daughter, my wife.
Obrigado, nós te amamos, muitas saudades nosso pai…

ACKNOWLEDGEMENTS

I love people!
God has graciously surrounded me with many glorious friends, dear brothers and sisters, and my precious family — Cristina, Benjamin and Joshua. God's treasures, that I get to enjoy on earth, and many for eternity.

I desire to thank the amazing Intel Bible-based Christian Network (IBCN) global team that I was involved with for 25 years. The Intel Cross-Faith Leaders of amazing friends with our conversations and prayers – Julia, Sarah, Alexander, May, Aaron, Hadi, Taz, and others (from the Atheist/Agnostic, Baha'i, Jew, Muslim, and Sikh groups). The Courageous Third Board: Greg, Becky, Mindy, Julia, and Greg. My close prayer partners and friends Kirsten and Heesung on the C3 Team. Raymond for opening the door for this trip. Brian Grim for his leadership in the Faith at Work arena. Roger our neighbor, encouraging me in his driveway at sunset to just follow Jesus. Dana for discipling our small group so many years ago, teaching me the discipline to follow God. The Lausanne Workplace volunteer team: Joseph, Bill, Jim, Judith, John, Joao.

My life is rich because of people.
God's eternal treasures on earth.

Some of the people I met during these 40 days and key friends that greatly impacted my life on this adventure: Abby, Abed, Adeline, Agata, Aka, Alina, Allen, Angela/Cesar, Anna, Ania, April, Ashley, Austin, Beatris, Benjie, Bethany, Bob, Brenda, Bruce, Cambridge, Chansamone, Carl, Charlene, Charlotte, Chris, Christy, Daisy, Dana, Dani, Daniel, David, Deborah, Denise, Derek, Diego, Dominic, Don, Doro, Dwayne, Edgar, Edward, Erin, Ezra, Florence, George, Glenn, Gloria, Grace, Gracie, Gabriela, Heather, Heesung, Heidi, Helena, Henrick, Henry, Heronima, Irina, Iwona, Jakub, Jan, Jayanthi, Jee-Hee,

Jeanie, Jenish, Jeremy, Jillian, Jim, Joesuan, Joseph, Josh, Judith, Judith, Jules, Karen, Kamal, Kamesh, Kathleen, Kennedy, Kent, Kevin, Kirsten, Lily, Lori, Lori Joe, Lorraine, Mahafahatra, Matthias, Marcelo, Mario, Mark, Markee, Maryum, Matt, May, Melissa, Melody, Meripeni, Michael, Mike, Mimi, Motoaki, Nadja, Natalia, Neala, Nicoletta, Pam, Paul, Peter, Pompey, Pramod, Putty, Quacy, Raymond, Roger, Ronald, Ruth, Sam, Sarah, Sayuri, Scott, Sean, Shah, Shannon, Srabanti, Stan, Steph, Stephen, Steve, Tadeusz, Taisiia, Terri, Theo, Timothy, Uday, Urszula, Vicky, Victoria, Vimbai, Vonjimlanla, Yitzchok, Yvonne. I am sure I have missed some close friends, and I apologize!

From countries where they live or were born:
Afghanistan, Bahamas, Brazil, Brunei, Canada, China, Costa Rica, Fiji, France, Germany, Guyana, India, Iran, Israel, Jamaica, Japan, Kazakhstan, Kenya, Lebanon, Liberia, Madagascar, Malaysia, Malta, Pakistan, Palestine, Philippines, Poland, Puerto Rico, Romania, Singapore, South Africa, Sweden, Switzerland, Taiwan, Texas :), Thailand, Uganda, Ukraine, USA, Vietnam, Zimbabwe.

God's children and friends are global, diverse, and amazing!

Thank you!
Knowing each of you fills my heart with joy.

Contents

Want the Best Life Ever?

you <u>must</u> follow me
JOHN 21:22

It's simple: **Just Follow.**

God has a sense of humor. All of this coming from someone holding roles like *Controller* and *Project Manager*, having spent 25 years progressively moving up and controlling my environment at a large global company. Ironically, it wasn't until God called me to surrender even more of my life, and in desperation I did, that my good life became the Best Life Ever.

You already are a follower, who are you following? This is the *most important decision* you will make in life. God gives us an invitation to have the best life ever, if we: Just Follow Him.

Beijing

I'll never forget the day standing in Tiananmen Square, surrounded by thousands, in a nation of 1.4 billion people in the heart of China. My heart had been transformed; it swelled with love for them all. I watched the crowds, smiling families, and thousands of cell phones capturing moments in time. Flags waved proudly, and women were adorned with heart-shaped stickers on cheeks that celebrated their national pride. Just the day before, I had been weeping alone in the room, overcome with emotion praying and fasting. I had asked God to fill me with all of His love — He did.

It was October 1, 2024 the 75th anniversary of the founding of the People's Republic of China, and I was in the middle of it. I was still in shock. A few days earlier, I had no idea I would be in Beijing or that it was even such a significant holiday on this exact day. When God said, *Go!* I followed. Now, I prayed as He desired me to, that His love would pour from the heavens, descending and sweep across the nation.

Washington D.C.

Fast forward a few weeks, and I found myself in another country, filled with joy, walking over 20,000 steps doing seven laps around the White House on a new prayer calling. This time, it was Washington D.C. on October 26, 2024 — just days before the contentious U.S. presidential election. God led me to fly there to pray, ordering me to not ask for anything, but only to rejoice in what He is doing. On the trip, where I had no plans to meet with anyone; God had other intentions. Meeting with former senior government leaders, prayed for many, and even met my new sister in Christ, Ruth, who is originally from Kenya and loves to pray like I do.

This kind of unexpected, joy-filled, adventurous life is becoming normal now. Something I've come to expect as part of a life of just following. It is just one more normal amazing day.

How does it feel?

It is the **Best Life Ever!**

Actual 40 Days

This book contains 40 actual days of my life, in the Fall of 2024, traveling to Korea, China, back home to Phoenix in the USA then to Washington D.C. What you will glimpse in these 40 days is normal for me, these sorts of things happen daily, and writing beyond 40 days would take up too much space. None of this is due to my expertise or wisdom, I only decided to say *yes* to just follow Him. You can do the same. The hope is this will paint a picture of the joy and challenge of following God. May it inspire you to join me on this journey. During these 40 days, I was blessed to closely connect with hundreds of individuals from dozens of nations. I listened to their stories, felt their pain and joy, wept with many, and prayed with basically all of them. The blessings God poured out on them (and me!) usually resulted in many tears and hugs, and always new friends. This deep love I could deliver and receive truly makes me the **richest person on earth!** The wealth of heaven presses down on me, with God's favor filling me, better than anything this world could offer. I want you to experience the same. Let me be blunt — just following God isn't easy. There's a very high price to pay to receive this incredible wealth from heaven. That's why so few choose this path. For a great return, there is a great cost.

Jesus warned us in the parable of the sower: most seeds don't bear fruit. Also, a seed must die to bear fruit. I strongly desire, with my whole life on the line, to be that seed that does bear much fruit, no matter what it takes. As Matthew 10:39 reminds us, *whoever loses their life for My sake will find it.* To follow, you must die to yourself, especially your will and desire to control. I've seen physical death up close — holding the hands of my father earlier in the year as he took his last breath. Death is painful. Surrendering your own will is no different. It will take amazing courage. However, the death and removal of your will is necessary for God to fill you completely. Removing your will is like unlocking the door for God to move in and to start His masterpiece building plan, with you being the masterpiece!

Stop Reading - only Continue if Courageous

If you want an ordinary life, you can stop reading now, read a different book or go watch a movie. However, if you want a life that overflows with purpose, joy, and impact — keep reading. The prize for following God is enormous!

This message is for the *Courageous Third.* Those choosing to be:

- *Courageous* — choosing to take action in spite of fear
- *Third* — putting God first, others second, and yourself third

Jesus was the perfect role-model of being the
Courageous Third

Jesus — the most influential, powerful, best leader, and the most loving person to have ever lived. He is our role model for the best life ever.

Likely only 1% of the readers will choose this path. Making it more selective than the best Universities in the world, and even more selective than elite military groups such as the U.S. Navy SEALs. You will be different from others, set apart, feel odd and alone at times, be confronted by immense fear and pain, yet you will also receive the BEST that God can offer. Trust me, it is better than you can imagine.

Ready to be Radical?

This book will challenge you. It will make you uncomfortable. I am full of weakness and countless failures daily, just like you. Nothing good dwells in me *(Romans 7:18)*, but God does, and He shines bright! What you will see though is a relentless drive to just follow Him. I'm opening the book of my life for you to see this journey. It's very personal, and it leaves me open to much criticism and with that pain. God told me to write this though, so I have to just follow. Please hold judgment until you see the fruit of my actions, it is an orchard full, praise God! My path and calling will definitely not be identical to yours, so don't just automatically try to copy all I do. God gives us immense freedom *(1 Corinthians 8:9)*, but my freedom may look different than yours. Where I can easily share God's love, you may fail or hurt people. Following God is following God first, no person or organization.

On this journey you will be transformed to love like Jesus, that is the common thread all followers of Christ have. Most struggle to receive this, it terrifies them. Men listen up. We men especially are challenged to love deeply, as it takes profound courage. Watch and learn from the ladies in your life, have courage like a girl! Be courageous, let God teach you how to love. There is no calling of God that does not rest on the foundation of profound merciful weeping powerful earth moving heaven shaking love. God created the heavens and the earth, that is awesome raw power. I want that! Yet, the single word best describing Him is love. God is LOVE. You want this. That is the best God has to offer, love.

Real and Raw

This text isn't a theory, a 10-step program, theological commentary or a philosophy; sheesh, I am a business guy that worked for a high-tech company! God calls us to shine the light of His love in the world, usually in the workplace, which is where I spent my life. In these pages you will see:

a wake of unexplainable God moments

All occurring as a weak man is on a journey of following God's path. Following God isn't just about surrendering your will — it's about dying to it. Yet, in that death, your treasured humanity — the person God created you to be — fully remains. God loves you! God even really likes you. Yes, truly, He likes you so much He wants to spend eternity with you, and wants to start now by walk with you. The Bible tells us, *He chose us in Him before the creation of the world (Ephesians 1:4).* As you follow, He will finish molding you into the powerful, beautiful, life-filled, blameless child of God you were always meant to be. You'll be transformed, filled with His love, walking with God's powerful authority, and equipped to love others.

God Likes you, Walk with Him!

God sees you as valuable. He died, so He could spend more time with you! He wants to shape you into a glorious masterpiece, to give you the **Best Life Ever**. He knows the way, and He patiently waits for us to choose to follow Him.

I am the way, the truth, and the life
I have come that they have abundant life
JOHN 14:6, 10:10

Do you want a full, abundant life?
A life of purpose, transforming the world?
Give up control. He knows the best way.

Just Follow

NOTES: Navigating the rest of the book.

- **Getting Ready.** *Prior to any journey you need to be prepared, a few bags packed, you will see these chapters at the front and throughout the book.*

- **Names changed.** *Where needed to protect people and shield their privacy, names and personally identifiable information has been changed. Personal information is of priceless value. I love each of these people. With many I will be with them for all eternity in heaven. That is a very long time, so I want them to smile every time they see me!*

- **Brothers and Sisters.** *You will see me say "brother or sister" over and over throughout the book. For those not familiar with the Christian culture and terms, I wanted to explain this. In the Bible, it tells us that other men and women that are also followers of Jesus are to be treated as our dear brothers and sisters. In 1 Timothy 5:1 it clearly says this:*
    "Treat younger men as brothers, older women as mothers,
       and younger women as sisters, with absolute purity"
  As followers of Jesus, we rarely do this, we are too busy or too fearful – not loving enough. We are disobedient to our calling to profoundly love. God is working on me to treat people as God desires me to.

- **Neighbors we Love.** *The Bible also tells us how we are to dearly love ALL people, as our close neighbors or family members. Read what Jesus himself taught in Luke 10:25-37, the story of the Good Samaritan. It was not the religious leader that loved like Jesus desired, it was the traveler, I assume a businessman :) that loved the person that was in need. Like with treating people as dear brothers and sisters, we rarely treat all we meet as a dear neighbor. God is working on my heart; may you choose to join me on this incredible journey.*

Chapter 1

Who are you? A Pastor?

you are a chosen people, a royal priesthood,
a holy nation, a people belonging to God
1 PETER 2:9

Jee-Hee was in tears, her voice shaking, looking at me and whispering, *I feel so blessed!* Overwhelmed with emotion, she could barely speak, unexpectedly feeling truly seen and cared for. We stood off to the side, near the table where she was volunteering at the Lausanne Korea conference. She and a coworker had been helping me find a place to store my luggage when God highlighted her to me. I had looked at her and simply asked, *How can I pray for you?*

Immediately, she stood up and suggested we move aside. She shared that the night before, she had broken up with her boyfriend, feeling they weren't pursuing God together as they should. She was about the same age as our two sons, my heart felt every word as I listened. After she shared, I prayed for her. With wide, tear-filled eyes, she asked the question I've heard so many times before, a question people always seem to ask in these moments. She didn't even know my name.

Who are you? Are you a pastor?

I had heard it countless times, and while I smiled back at her, inside I felt that familiar frustration rising. *Really?* I thought. *In the Body of Christ, is the only person people expect to listen and pray for them an ordained pastor or priest? No wonder the world is hurting. We, as followers of Christ, have a problem here.* God calls all of us to minister to others and to love as Christ loves. No exceptions. Think of a sports stadium. There are only four places to be.

- **Outside:** not yet part of God's family

Inside the stadium, part of God's family as a…
- **Spectator:** watching, glad to be in, but not helping
- **Coach:** critical role to support and train the athletes
- **Athlete:** those engaged directly with the sport

Athletes: Front-Line Ministers at Work

That's you, the athletes, the 99% who work. In Korea I meet Helena, a pediatrician from Brazil. She was thinking of leaving medicine as she felt called to become a full-time minister. We talked; she will not leave medicine. She realized she can best serve God in this beautiful role of loving children and their parents as a doctor. She is a front-line and a full-time minister, at work. Most of God's children are not employed by religious institutions. They are out in the world — making, serving, consulting, and working. I am asked so often if I am a pastor that I finally developed a response, you and I are:

Working Ministers - Reflecting God's Love @ Work.

This is where ministry happens. I am biased, as the world of work is where I live, but I believe this is the best place to show the love of God. It is the playing field; *you are the athlete on it.*

A number of years ago I was at an evening meeting with about 200 men. The group met weekly for an in-depth Bible study. They invited a man to come forward, for us to pray for him. He announced that after 20 years at Intel Corporation, he was leaving his engineering role to enter, *full-time Christian ministry*. I was shocked, I knew him! He worked for years in the same building as me, and I never knew he was a Jesus follower. The man was not engaged in the Christian community at Intel, never having been involved in his 20 years there. As the room prayed for him, I wanted to weep, saddened and crying out to God. Another front-line minister, leaving his strategic position on the field of play, to go into *full-time Christian ministry?* God has called us all to full-time ministry, especially you, God's *athletes* called to the challenging front-lines of work.

Coaching and Support Staff: Clergy

For the 1% who are paid and trained clergy, pastors, priests, you are the coaches and trainers, equipping the athletes on the field, for the work of ministry. Think of any sports team — without a coach, the team fails. Everything must support equipping the saints to be the light of Jesus in the world, *(Ephesians 4:12)*. Those of us on the front lines — working in offices, schools, shops, or wherever our daily lives take us — are daily engaged with the world, to be His loving light. We need your guidance, encouragement, example, and prayers. You are the support team that helps us succeed.

Many pastors, priests, and clergy don't see themselves as coaches, trainers, or equippers for those at work. This isn't intentional, as they have beautiful hearts! They spend years studying in seminary, then most go directly into a religious organization. They just don't understand. Most have never spent year after year, decade after decade being a minority in a secular workplace, facing a daily battle where their beliefs are challenged and unwelcome. A coach must understand the athletes under their care, who spend 55% of their waking hours at work. Yes, over half of a person's life, is spent at work!

We need clergy to enter this at times *scary* world of work and understand the daily battle. Work is dirty, tough, risky, unpredictable — and at times will require breaking tradition. Jesus spent most of His time here. Of Jesus' 132 appearances, 93% of them, 122 times, were not in a church *(thank you Mark Whitacre!)*. Those in the workplace need courageous clergy.

You are raising up ministers in the workplace. Most front-line ministers are discouraged, weary, and unsure how to fulfill their calling in environments that feel so foreign to their faith. They live divided lives, often feel like hypocrites, where faith and work are separated by a huge wall. Please equip us.

Help us tear down this wall

All of us who are believers in Jesus are a: **Pastor and a Priest**

As you saw with Jee-Hee, the world needs love.
Go and minister to them!

Chapter 2

My Journey:
Controller to Follower

"Come, follow me" Jesus said
JOHN 8:12

*G*o to Brazil and live there for a year, get a job and learn Portuguese, *you save a lot and have enough money, I will get you the visa.* That was what I heard God tell me about 30 years ago, glad I obeyed! That obedience led me to marrying my Brazilian pen-pal, *YES*! This path of radically following God goes back decades, with God consistently asking me to trust Him more as He leads me to do ever larger and larger acts requiring trusting obedience. Thankfully God is gracious, and increases our faith slowly! Here is some of my background, as it will provide context, and it may surprise you. I have been happily married for 30 years to my precious Brazilian pen-pal, who is beyond a rich blessing from God in my life, My Ruby. God also blessed us with two sons we are very close to, both now in college. We have lived in Phoenix, Arizona, USA for almost 30 years – next to a desert mountain range where I love to go spend quiet time with God. My family is my greatest blessing from God on this earth, a source of love, joy, and purpose. Through my journey, God has challenged me to even place this treasure at His feet, so I can fulfill my ultimate calling – to follow God.

Professional Career

Professionally, I spent over 25 years at Intel Corporation, working across various roles in international business – Corporate Finance Controller, Project Manager, Product

Manager, Buyer, and Strategist. With an undergraduate degree in Finance and a Master's in International Management from Thunderbird. I was constantly drawn to teams exploring new ideas and initiatives. I loved managing and took great pride in building the most productive and fun-loving teams at Intel. Over the 25 years, it felt like God was slowly increasing my ability to shine His love at work. It was peaking the last few years at Intel being able to pray for 10 or more people a week, often at the end of 1:1 meetings with people from every faith. A very special opportunity was a few months prior to leaving, when I was having a work meeting with a younger product manager originally from India. He was very nervous, as he was concerned he may lose his job, as the company was reducing headcount. This could force him to move his family and newly born daughter from the USA back to India. During the video call, I asked him why he had a painted dot on his forehead, he said it was for a Hindu religious festival happening that week. At the end of the call, I asked if I could pray for him, he was overjoyed – and I prayed. After praying he asked if I could be a father figure to him and if we could stay connected even after I left Intel. Amen! We are called to reflect God's love at work, to everyone!

Leading through Faith at Intel

One of my greatest privileges was leading the *Intel Christian Employee Resource Group, called IBCN (Intel Bible-based Christian Network)*. Through God's blessing, this group grew from being present in three nations to being in 23 countries, with over 4,000 members, including locations in China, Vietnam, India, Israel, and other countries. In some countries it was reclassified as a club due to legal restrictions. Intel had Christian groups in 3 countries for over 20 years, then we started praying, and that is when the growth started! The many stories of blessing, from just this Christian group, could fill a whole book. As this growth was happening, God pushed me to start the *Intel Cross-Faith Leaders Group* – a space for leaders from various faiths, including Atheist/Agnostic, Baha'i, Christian, Hindu, Jewish, Muslim, and Sikh communities. I do not always follow God, and initially when He asked me to do this, I told Him, *No!* for three days in a row, as I would not compromise my faith. In the words of the Christian leader at Amazon, she said *Craig, so you were sure you had heard God's command, and you told Him 'No!' three days in a row? I have never heard of a dumber person than you!* I had never thought of it that way, she was right! On the fourth day, when God's requesting tone changed, it compelled me in fear to start it, I am glad I did! With no compromise to my or any faith, this Cross-Faith group seeded some of the most amazing and wonderful friendships I have ever been in, all with no compromise to any faith or belief. Doors were opened to bless the other leaders, praying for most of them, and many I have stayed in contact with and consider dear friends. The Cross-Faith initiative was instrumental in Intel Corporation becoming #1 in the world for Religious Inclusion, earning the United Nations Gold Medal award and recognition in global indexes *(www.religiousfreedomandbusiness.org).*

Through this work, I was blessed to connect with Christian and other faith leaders at many Fortune 500 companies including: Amazon, GE, Microsoft, American Airlines, American Express, ExxonMobil, Cargill, Disney, Meijer, Coca-Cola and many others. In the summer of 2022 when in prayer, God made it clear that my time at Intel was coming to an end. Exactly 4 weeks later, I was offered a severance package and retirement, which marked the beginning of a new chapter starting in 2023. With great anticipation, I left the stable 25-year career and entered a new adventure of following.

The Power of Being Different

One of the most impactful lessons I learned from God is that being different can create opportunities. This realization came when we organized an annual reading of Martin Luther King Jr.'s (MLK) speeches, with readers from diverse backgrounds. A significant moment was when a speaker from Asia recited the final lines of the *I Have a Dream* speech with passion and a thick accent: *Free at last, free at last, thank God almighty, we are free at last!* Her delivery moved the audience of over 200 people to tears, leading to a standing ovation. This initiative began nearly a decade ago when Intel granted employees a holiday for the MLK Day. Having little knowledge of MLK's life, I read his book *Strength to Love*, and his focus on unity, love, and character greatly moved me. I felt compelled by God to share his message at work, despite my initial hesitation. Eventually, I approached a colleague from the DEI: Diversity, Equity, and Inclusion team, who questioned why I, a white man, wanted to read MLK's speech. I responded that MLK's message transcends race and is about love and unity, we all need this.

The first reading, with 120 attendees, was a success, and the annual event now is in its 8th year at many US locations and also globally. It now features over 40 readers, including Intel's CEO and senior leaders from Microsoft, with thousands of employees tuning in. When you love someone not like yourself, being different, it is powerful and is a multiplier of blessings.

From Controller to Follower

My work titles — Controller, Project Manager — describe my natural personality. I like to be in control. Yet in the years since leaving Intel, God has been teaching me the hardest yet most fulfilling lesson: to die to control and to just follow. A friend, urged me to reflect on Matthew 10, where Jesus calls us to put Him above everything. This is where you start to realize the potential cost of being a follower. To just follow is not easy, it will be the hardest thing you do in life. Let me say it bluntly:

*there is NOTHING **harder** than following God*

*there is NOTHING **more satisfying** than following God*

The words from Matthew 10, Mark 10 and Luke 14, Luke 18 are painfully real to me, yet also are full of glorious joy.

Anyone who loves father, mother, wife, son, daughter, home or wealth more than me, is not worthy of me. And anyone who does not take up his cross and follow me is not worthy of me. Whoever finds his life will lose it, and whoever loses his life for my sake will find it. Those that follow will not fail to receive a hundred times as much… (paraphrased)

I have lost control, but… **I have gained LIFE**.
It was a good exchange. I now just follow.

Chapter 3

Courageous Third

*I believe that one of the next great moves of God
is going to be through the believers in the workplace.*
-BILLY GRAHAM

*Work makes the human person similar to God…
a creator.*
-POPE FRANCIS

The vision started before I left Intel. It has been discussed with hundreds of global workplace leaders. *Courageous Third*, a global ultra-secure community to transform the world through giving people an amazing life at work, where we spend 55% of our waking hours.

Courageous Third
LinkedIn for Jesus Followers @Work

What is Courageous Third?

As we follow, we must be Courageous and Third. These two words have resonated with hundreds of Christian workplace leaders in large companies such as Intel, American Express, American Airlines, Ford, Zurich Insurance, United Health Care, Amazon and so many others.

- *Courageous*: taking action in spite of fear.
- *Third*: putting God first, others second, yourself third.

As we lean into being the *Courageous Third*, we will naturally *Reflect God's Love @Work*, giving us and others the best life ever. It is about reflecting God's love, the world not seeing us, but Him in our life. That is what transforms people and the world.

Value: For Me, For the World
The target audience is all Jesus followers globally that work (1 billion). As they become:

Courageous and Third, Reflecting God's Love @Work

People and the world receive tremendous value.
- **For Me (and you!)**: coming Fully Alive! The best life ever, as we have real relationships and purpose at work, where 55% of life happens.
- **For the World**: tasting God's love, it will be transformed: you → organizations → nations → world

What do People Want?
A better life at work! Desperately desiring to be:

Connected + Inspired + Equipped + Protected

The Courageous Third solution will create this through real community at work, leveraging AI to provide personalized spiritual growth plans and inform users how they can benefit from the thousands of ministries that already exist. Peer to peer networking and recent technology is teaching us how to create ultra-secure global solutions.

Other factors and FAQs:
- **Current Social Media platforms are not sufficient:** they are never used to manage large workplace Christian groups. They are not made for this, and they are not trusted.
- **Protection of the Data is key:** people do not trust current platforms or Corporate HR. It has to exist outside the company walls, and be ultra-secure.
- **Non-Profit structure, focus on the value to users, not for profit** as it needs to be different from Meta, LinkedIn, etc. It must be highly trusted to make recommendations to benefit the users, not advertisers, businesses or ministries.

- **The time is NOW!** The technology is ready, people are hungry for *Real Relationships @Work*, the world is in pain.

Just Follow – God's timing is better

Two years before I left Intel, Nicoleta a friend who lives a life of prayer in Switzerland, shared a vision with me that I still remember well.

> *I was in prayer. I saw you as if you were a racehorse, in the starting gate. Panting, sweating, muscles ready to run on the race track. Yet the gate would not open and you were very frustrated. Then I saw what was out on the track, huge horrifying monsters with multiple heads that were ready to consume you, kill you, crush you, and you didn't see them at all. You thought you were ready. God, however knows you are not, and is not allowing you to run yet. In time you will be ready, then the gate will open and you will run.*

This image struck me, glad I didn't race down that track! Looking back now, God had much work to do in my heart. Teaching me to depend fully on Him and to realize my dependence on others. God has asked me to travel significantly, meet many different people, and learn how to *Just Follow*. I thought I was a good loving follower of Christ; I didn't realize how much I still had to learn.

God changing my heart, I have realized, is of the highest importance to Him, not what I do. His love for me, and His desire for me to walk closely with Him is His paramount desire, now it is also mine. **I will walk Courageous and Third**.

If you would like more information, visit us at:

www.ReadCraigCarter.com

COURAGEOUS THIRD
Reflecting God's LOVE @Work

Chapter 4

Not All Hear

The Lord had said to Abram,
"Go from your country, your people and
your father's household to the land I will show you."
GENESIS 12:1

I felt God urging me to travel to Asia for three weeks, visiting South Korea and China. To attend two conferences in South Korea, and to visit Christian friends in China. The Sunday before the trip, I couldn't sleep. At 1:20AM, the phrase *ambassador in chains* from Ephesians 6 kept echoing in my mind. Not words you desire to hear just prior to a big trip! Paul's words about spiritual warfare and being a servant of God, being fully surrendered to His will, resonated with me. Abraham was called by God to follow, and nowhere in the Bible does it record that his wife or family heard the call, Abraham alone had heard God and he had been commanded to follow. Can you imagine the hard dinner conversations Abraham had!

The night before had been difficult for my wife and I. She was uncomfortable with my travel plans, especially to China, and felt that three weeks was just too long. She had good reasons—this year had been full of unexpected changes, both wonderful and painful. Our youngest son had graduated from high school, leaving us as empty nesters, and in the same month, my father died unexpectedly. The aftermath of his death brought painful family tensions. Meanwhile, I had traveled multiple times unexpectedly and wasn't bringing home a paycheck, which only added to the instability at home. On top of this, I was mentoring many people, pouring into their lives, which made my wife feel that my attention was divided and not just focused on our family.

Jesus, I Trust You

1:30AM I was in the living room, on my knees praying and feeling sick. My wife, my treasure, was hurting, and I felt awful. I kept thinking of the Polish phrase from a painting of Jesus I had seen in Poland:

Jezu Ufam Tobie – Jesus, I trust You

I stared at a small reproduction of the painting, called *Divine Mercy*, and prayed, heartbroken for both myself and my wife. She had every reason to oppose the trip, and I wrestled with whether I was neglecting my responsibility as her husband. Mark 6:50-52, where the disciples' hearts were hardened, came to mind, and I questioned whether I was like them, failing to see what Jesus was trying to show me.

Then I saw a note in my Bible from over a year ago, on that same page by Mark 6:50-52, when I had been in Rome: *Lord, give me your love, your soft heart.* God had answered that prayer earlier in the year, just 6 months prior, during a trip to Krakow, Poland, to pray. That trip had transformed my heart, and given me friends that sincerely pray for me. By seeing that little note in my Bible, I was reminded how God was in control of everything.

As I prayed on my knees at home, on the carpet in the middle of the night, I remembered the vow on my knees on cold cobblestones in St. Peter's Square in Rome over a year prior:

Lord, I will go where You want me to go.

I will do what You want me to do.

With that memory and oath to God, peace washed over me. God had clearly called me to this trip, and I would follow, just as Paul had followed as an *ambassador in chains*. There was no alternative. I would go where He wanted me to, even if no one else heard or understood His call. I felt a bit like Abraham, hearing a calling that His family did not hear. With that decision, I returned to bed, at peace.

Chapter 5

Prayer Mountain: Korea (Day 1)

여호와의 성령께서 나를 통해 말씀 하시니 그의 말씀이 내 혀에 있구나.
2 SAMUEL 23:2 (IN KOREAN)

God called me to travel to Asia early, to spend time in prayer. So I arrived in Seoul, South Korea a few days before the large Lausanne Conference that started in late September of 2024. I didn't know where I would be praying, but I trusted that God would provide a place. He always does when we follow. I landed late Thursday, and today was Friday morning, I was on a 2-hour taxi ride to Osanri Prayer Mountain. This massive prayer complex, was built by the Yoido Full Gospel Church, which I believe is the largest Protestant church in the world. With over 500,000 members, the church built a separate prayer facility, *Prayer Mountain*, with space that can accommodate up to 20,000 people and with over 100 individual prayer rooms, it's truly remarkable.

Earlier that week, just four days before, I had learned about this place in an unexpected way. It came from Helena, a Korean woman I briefly met at a Chicago conference two years ago, who sends me daily Bible verses. When I texted her to ask where in Korea I could pray for an entire day, she immediately suggested Osanri Prayer Mountain. It was another example of how God uses others to guide us.

When I arrived, I sat in the sanctuary and thought, *this is no small prayer chapel!* The sanctuary could easily hold thousands, though the attendance ranged the day I was there from 200 to maybe 1000. The location is always open for prayer, 24 hours a day, 365 days a year. The atmosphere was saturated with God's presence. Although I couldn't understand a word of the Korean services, I could feel the Holy Spirit at work. Between the services, the lights dimmed, and soft worship music played. Along with about 200 other people, I prayed, completely immersed in God's presence. The Spirit moved through me, bringing name after name to my mind. I prayed for each person, sometimes standing, sometimes sitting, as if I were physically with them.

After this intense time of prayer, I felt a tap on my left shoulder. A smiling lady, who had been sitting behind me, handed me a piece of paper with something written in Korean. Using an app on my phone to translate, it was 2 Samuel 23:2

여호와의 성령께서나를 통해 말씀 하시니그의 말씀이

내 혀에 있구나.

The Spirit of the Lord spoke through me; his word was on my tongue

After giving me the paper, she smiled again and left. I sat there, overwhelmed and in awe of what God had done, pondering what this meant for the three weeks ahead in Asia. This was just the beginning.

During the last service at Prayer Mountain, I moved to the front row. Even though the songs were in Korean, I recognized the tune to the old hymn *Power in the Blood*. I felt led to go to the front and kneel in worship, in the middle of my Korean brothers and sisters, feeling the presence of the Holy Spirit powerfully. That hymn marked the end of the first full day and my time at Prayer Mountain, but it was only the beginning of what God had in store. Little did I know that at the end of the 40-day journey, I would hear the same hymn again in a black Pentecostal church by Washington D.C., as people danced and waved flags in worship. God's ways are truly wonderful and point to how He orchestrates even little things.

He is so fully in control; I can trust Him.

These sorts of realizations just increase my faith in Him, and my desire and capability to follow Him well. Keep your eyes open, He is always doing something miraculous!

Bus and a Prayer

At Prayer Mountain, I prayed for the upcoming presidential election, asking that the candidate who would advance God's will be lifted up, and the other brought down. As I took the shuttle bus back to the city, I reflected on the amazing day immersed in prayer, while sitting next to Pastor Kevin from Africa. Upon arriving in the city, another woman I had seen at the prayer service approached me. Using her phone to translate, she asked if I was a pastor and when I would return to Korea. These encounters made me smile and know I was on the right path; God's light was reflecting off of me. It did make me ponder again on how people often assume a person is ordained clergy, a pastor or priest, when they see a person immersed in prayer. We are all pastors, ministers to the world.

After the bus ride, Kevin and I shared a taxi ride to the hotel. He opened up about personal struggles he had never shared with others prior. I felt blessed to listen, encourage, and pray for him, holding his hand as we prayed together in the back of the taxi. That ride, which took four hours between the bus and the taxi, was all about connecting with and blessing Kevin. We, as the body of Christ, need each other.

Preparation for the rest of the book

You will see what just happened with Kevin repeated many times. Get ready for lots of prayer and hearts being touched! Two people coming together, with God in the middle, and the result is lives are wonderfully transformed with the love of God. Jesus tells us in Matthew 18:20:

> *For where two or three come together in my name,*
> *there am I with them.*

This verse is reality! God, the Creator of all things, is with us when we pray together! This is what you are seeing. It is not me that you should see much of; as I am a weak man that struggles to fully just follow Him. What the focus should be on is the glorious wonder of an infinite God partnering with us finite beings to incredibly touch hearts in the most special, caring and profound ways. There are three parties involved; God, me (or you), and the recipient. A key part is the heart stance of the person receiving the prayer. They have to desire His touch. Most people want this, but be prepared, a few do not. It is rare that someone does not want to feel the love of God, but this occurred just a month ago when I was at our small church. I felt I should pray for a man during the singing, I did, he thanked me and gave me a hug. After the singing I asked him if I could pray for him more, he looked at me strangely and responded, *I am good, no need*, and turned his back and walked to get coffee. That puzzled me and I asked God if I had made a mistake asking him. I felt God say, what I did was His desire, but it still made me wonder. Later that day, as the pastor was talking, this man raised his hand and started to make very strange occult-like comments, puzzling the pastor and the whole church. It was then I realized, that not all desire, or are able, to receive the touch and love of God. However, this is very rare, most people, believers in Jesus or not – desperately want to be seen and loved, so move forward, pray!

This close partnership with God only occurs when we choose to follow Him, united at His side following.

The amount of love we show others
is directly proportional to how closely we walk with God.

We have to receive His love to give it away. Following Him aligns us to accept His love. Think of it as though we are a cup. As we follow Him closely, we are now perfectly positioned under the waterfall of God's love! As His love fills us, we naturally overflow, and pour it into their dry hearts. It is glorious, and fills us also, flowing through us to others! My desire is you experience this best life.

Think of a cross, Jesus' arms were pinned to that torturous structure, arms open, to embrace us closely in His love. Accept His embrace, His divine hug. He paid a huge price, an excruciating painful death, to just hug you tightly—please do not reject Him. You will receive His love and the courage to just follow Him, giving you the best life. Jesus tells us He knows the path. In these pages you will see this journey lived out, a life of abundant blessing, overflowing with love, even in the middle of piercing pain, Jesus says:

I am the way, the truth, and the life
I have come that they have abundant life
JOHN 14:6, 10:10

He is God, He knows the path, we do not! What you will see is *normal* from God's perspective. What God intended for all of His children, yet we rarely see it. May you join me on this journey of following God.

Following God though does take effort as this day showed! I was in buses and taxis for almost 6 hours during this day. Was it worth it? Of course it was! With all these experiences echoing in my heart, I went to sleep, filled with awe of what God had already done — and with anticipation for what was still to come. It was only the first full day. I drifted off to sleep thinking of the words the Korean Lady had written to me on the paper, and I prayed asking God to speak through me to bless many.

God hears.
He would answer that prayer.

Chapter 6

Prayers of the Saints

They all joined together constantly in prayer,
along with the women and Mary, the mother of Jesus
and with his brothers.
ACTS 1:14

Before my trip, my wife, sons, friends from church, and many colleagues from around the world reached out to me, offering to pray. While it's nice when someone says they'll pray for you, it doesn't carry much weight for me. When someone takes the time to pray with you on the spot or arranges a prayer meeting, that's when I feel the true power of prayer and love. If you do this, you'll see eyes light up in surprise as you bless them with prayer. Don't put off prayer!

I've been privileged to pray for people from all backgrounds, nationalities, and walks of life—young, old, men, women, believers in Jesus and those that do not know Jesus yet. From my experience, over 99% see it as a rich blessing to be prayed for. Do not shrink back in fear because of the 1% that will not like it! At work, I learned from friends in Human Resources, even when the company would give employees an extra paid holiday, there are a few employees who always complain. So, my advice: pray for people whenever you can!

At our small church, before I traveled, they called me forward and the church prayed for me, sending me off like the early apostles as a representative of Christ in Asia. It was a profound experience—my first time being prayed over by the entire congregation before a trip. I truly felt anointed, filled with God's presence and favor.

Two men from the church also prayed for me separately, yet both had the same message: I need to be bold in prayer, confident in the authority of God, as His ambassador on this journey. I could feel God's power behind me, equipping me for the task. It was clear that I wasn't going alone—God was sending me with His full backing. It was through the voice and hands of His people that it was communicated to me. We need each other. The saints do this as a team. We all are saints, of course! As Paul the Apostle tells us in Romans 1:7, *To all those in Rome who are loved by God and called to be saints.*

About a month before the trip, two people prayed over me with powerful words of prophecy. One shared a vision of seeing me as a spear, my words piercing hearts and influencing people in positions of power. They saw me separated from things I held dear, but assured me I'd be reunited with them in time, as God was in control. I was likened to a small organism placed by God into a vast sphere of power—an area I could never reach by my own efforts. This vision was about how my life would be used for transformation in this sphere, from the inside out, that I would go unnoticed, in stealth, until the time was right. It was a profound word about how God would use me in a place I could never have entered on my own. These sorts of words lifted me up, encouraging me to walk forward.

God Speaks to Us Through Others.

We are fully dependent on both God and His Body—the Church. I like to say this, as I always get raised eyebrows.
God is not enough for me...

I also need His Body. This was always His plan, as His Body is part of Him (of course!). The wonderful alone time with Him is not enough, I need to be in close loving relationship with His entire global Body, His children, His Church. We cannot do His work alone; we need each other, working together like different parts of the same body. Do all of His children agree on everything? Do my beloved wife of 30 years and I agree on everything? You know the answer. So, we must focus on what unites us, not the differences. Jesus often spoke of His desire for us to be united, working in harmony for His purposes. Please ponder on this. Many try to do life alone, saying *God alone is enough*. To reach the finish line, we run it with God's other kids, and it is so much more fun to win as a team!

My wife and sons also prayed over me at home before I left. It was a brief heartfelt prayer time heavily focused on my protection—asking that I remain unnoticed while accomplishing everything God had planned for me. It made me feel loved and supported.

Just before my departure, two dear friends from our Courageous Third team held an hour-long dedicated prayer meeting for me prior to the Asia travels. That's caring love. In that meeting, they prayed for God to mold me and empower me with His authority for His glory. We also prayed together, asking for God's love to consume us, because love is the greatest of all things. 1 Corinthians 13 reminds us that while wisdom, healing, and miraculous powers are important, nothing compares to the value of love. It is the foundation of all we do in His name. One friend was led to pray Psalm 24 over me:

...Who may ascend the hill of the Lord? Who may stand in his holy place? He who has clean hands and a pure heart... He will receive blessing from the Lord, and vindication from God his Savior... Lift up your heads, O you gates; be lifted up, you ancient doors, that the King of glory may come in.

That prayer reminded me that I was being called to climb the mountain of the Lord, to be blessed, and to open the gates for the King of glory to come through. It was humbling and inspiring, preparing me for what lay ahead. What added to this powerful prayer time was that my friend who prayed Psalm 24 didn't even know that I would be going to a place called *Prayer Mountain* to pray. Amen!

A Polish friend from Europe, also prayed Psalm 91 over me for the trip. The prayer called for God's protection, that He would shelter and hide me from evil. The final lines of the Psalm touched my heart:

Because he loves me, says the Lord, I will rescue him; I will protect him, for he acknowledges my name. He will call on me, and I will answer him; I will be with him in trouble, I will

*deliver him and honor him. With long life, I will satisfy him
and show him my salvation.*

Looking back, all these prayers, words of encouragement, and prophecies led to incredible God moments during the trip. It's amazing how God works in ways we can't always see or understand at the time. A friend at work once told me,

God doesn't make mistakes.
Everything that happens to you has a purpose.

That was comforting, especially during some tough times that would soon come.

You are Part of a Body – Act like it!

God hears our prayers, and He invites us to join Him in His grand plan. We aren't called to walk alone — we are part of His body, the Body of Christ. Amazing things happen when we unite and work together in His name. So run toward your family, your fellow believers! We belong to each other as members of Christ's body. As Romans 12:5 reminds us:

...so in Christ, we who are many form one body,
*and each member **belongs** to all the others.*

They belong to you.
You belong to them.
Pray with them!

Chapter 7

A Slave of All
(Day 2)

whoever wants to be first must be slave of all
MARK 10:44

I've always been drawn to leadership. From playing with friends as a child, to business, to volunteering. I see myself as a strong caring leader, having built and managed diverse global teams at Intel and led large complex global volunteer groups. Put me in front of a microphone with a room full of people, and I feel right at home! For the conference, I was facilitating the all-volunteer team organizing the speakers, for the Lausanne Workplace Track. I had not been asked to speak, which surprised me. God made it abundantly clear to me that I had internal pride that needed to be dealt with. My role for this conference was to serve and lift up the others with all of my strength, holding nothing back.

That morning, as I read my Bible, God reminded me of His desire for me: to serve others fully, meet their needs, not to take, but to give. I prayed, *Lord Jesus, help me, because I'm not naturally wired this way. I want to love like this, but I need your help!* God heard my prayer. As my wife often reminds me when I pray for things, *Honey, be careful what you pray for – it will happen!*

During these 40 days, I was blessed to serve and bless hundreds, then He did decide to lift me up. I realized that loving and helping others is such a rich blessing—both to them and to me. It beyond fills me up! There's truly nothing more fulfilling than serving those God places in our life, nothing!

Early that morning, while working out in the hotel gym, I met Nathan, a large man from Belgium, clearly training to recover from a knee injury. I had the privilege of putting my hands on his knee and praying for his healing. Then, at breakfast, I saw Judith from Jamaica for the first time. After countless volunteer team video calls, we finally met face to face, and I gave her a big hug. She texted our team later, saying, *I finally met Craig, and he gave me a huge hug – it was the best!* It's amazing how a little care can touch people's hearts. To do so effectively requires sensitivity to God's leading, as we can't always know what others need.

The Platinum Rule

I was reminded of a powerful statement I heard from Josh, who led a Christian employee group at his large company:

> *The golden rule tells us to love others as we would want to be loved. But the higher **Platinum Rule** calls us to love them in the way they, not we, would like to receive love. This of course is what Jesus meant, and we need to do it, following the platinum rule takes insight into their heart.*

This came to mind when I read Judith's text. That hug meant more to her than I ever could have imagined. It was the platinum rule in action, and it could only have happened through God's guidance. How blessed I felt – just following God's lead and opening the door for His love to flow through me to Judith.

Blessing and Tilling the Soil

God's blessings continued to unfold. At breakfast, I felt led to sit next to Damian, a pastor involved with Baptist efforts in Brazil, a place I had lived for a year. We spoke in Portuguese, and I was blessed by his story and struggles. Over video I could even say hello to his family. We prayed for each other at the breakfast table, and I could see how much it meant to him. I love breakfast, but breakfast with prayer is even better!

Throughout the conference, I experienced the fruit of serving others, having helped some speakers out for months prior. I spoke with speakers like Jala from Uganda, Mandisa from

Madagascar, and others, who shared how my encouragement and prayers had been instrumental to them deciding to attend the conference. What a profound blessing to witness the impact of serving God's people! Jesus was right—it truly is more blessed to give than to receive.

As the day came to a close, I walked over to the convention center, exploring and praying as I went. After some searching, I found the enormous room where we would host the Workplace Track, with seating for 1,500 attendees, with over 200 tables. It was awe-inspiring. I walked the room, circling the room in prayer. Then standing on the stage, I prayed and read Psalm 24, feeling the area wet with prayer. The same Psalm my friend had been led to pray over me a few days prior.

That room was prepared fertile wet ground, and I knew miracles would take root there. They would.

Chapter 8

Woman Roommate? (Day 3)

John's... food was locusts and wild honey.
MATTHEW 3:4

*my servant Isaiah has gone stripped and barefoot
for three years as a sign*
ISAIAH 20:3

Be ready for the unexpected when following God!
Just hope it is not eating locusts or going without clothes!

It was Saturday night when I checked into a new hotel — the one where I'd be staying for the week of the conference. The hotel was more like an apartment, the room was on the 15th floor. It had a small kitchen, a bed, and an open loft upstairs with a bed and a very low ceiling. I had just dropped my bags in the room and went out looking for dinner. My assigned roommate was Timothy, who was obviously not there yet. Upon returning, I entered the crowded elevator and was surprised to see Timothy, my roommate, standing right in front of me. I happily started talking to him, but he was silent, a worried look on his face. We stepped out of the elevator together, and I opened the door to our room, inviting him in.

To my surprise, he did not walk toward me, but stood outside the door, talking to an older woman next to a few suitcases. With a sad expression, he introduced her as his mother, Judith. *Her hotel room didn't work out,* he explained, *and now she had nowhere to stay.* Without hesitation, I invited Judith

45

to stay in our room for the night. They could share the bed downstairs, and I would sleep in the loft. They were incredibly grateful and amazed by the offer.

Judith and Timothy are from the Bahamas, and had just arrived in Korea. They were clearly hungry, so giving them my dinner sandwich, I quickly left to buy more food. Oh, how God orchestrates every detail, as little did I know, others were also hungry and that God would use me to feed them. On the way down, I met two men from Africa who had just arrived, so I invited them to join me at Burger King—I wasn't up for figuring out Korean food at that late hour. On our way, we walked by two women, one from Pakistan and the other from Bangladesh. None of them had local currency or credit cards, so I paid for their meals. The women, embarrassed by the offer, declined, but the men were happy to join me for hamburgers. The reality of this situation hit me again, I am blessed financially, and I am thankful.

When I returned to the room, I found Judith in her pink pajamas, sitting on the bed with her son Timothy. They were both very thankful for the sandwich and for the place to stay. As we spoke, I learned more about Judith and her family. She was the mother of seven boys, and she felt a calling to pray for people and to minister to men—a calling that resonated with me, as I feel called to minister to and uplift women. Her story was incredible: she had spent much of her life raising her seven sons on her own, after separating from her husband. She travels the world to pray at a moment's notice, following God's direction without a clear plan or fully knowing why—just following.

A Gift: A Mother

Judith said she heard God tell her to travel to Korea on a similar mission—to pray for someone and bless them. Little did she or I know, that I was one of the ones she was meant to bless. Over the course of the week, I grew closer to Judith, Timothy, and another son, Peter, who arrived later. Every morning, we would gather to pray together. Judith adopted me as her eighth son, the oldest. We may have looked different—she had dark skin, and I was light-skinned — but we shared the same Spirit. I love Judith my dear mother and her boys so much.

One morning, I felt led to pray for Judith and anoint her feet with oil I had brought with me from Jerusalem, where I had traveled the year prior. I asked her if she would allow me to do this, and she agreed without hesitation. As she sat there on the bed in her pink pajamas with legs outstretched, I knelt and prayed over her feet. I wept, as God used me to show Judith His great love for her. Her two sons stood behind me, laying their hands on my shoulders as I prayed. We all had a group hug afterward, immersed in the tender loving presence of God. As I anointed her feet with oil, I saw Judith dressed as if a beautiful bride in a royal white dress, adorned with flowers in her hair, smiling brightly. This was how God saw her, and it was how I saw her too.

Judith, with tears in her eyes, praised God. After I finished praying, she prayed for me, blessing me with words of encouragement about my future ministry, a future role in the US Government she was sure I would have, my marriage, my calling to support women, and racial healing. Then, she gave me the warmest, most loving mommy hug. I needed that hug. We all embraced as a new family — a white man in a dark-skinned family — and it felt like nothing less than divine. Judith, who is the exact age of my mother, became a spiritual mother to me. What a glorious and very unexpected gift!

A few months prior, I had lost my father unexpectedly, and the relationship with my extended family had been strained. I was wounded deeply. God knew this, and called Judith from the Bahamas all the way to Korea to pour God's love into my heart. Through Judith, her words and hands were used by God to tenderly heal that wound. She prayed over me from Philippians 1 and 4, and I felt the love of God surround me in a way that encircled me with protection and hope.

Racial Wounds

When young, I grew up in northern Montana, in the USA, where everyone looked like me, white. I had never experienced racial prejudice, and the pain that comes from it. The concept had seemed foreign to me, and hard to understand as I never grew up seeing it. That morning changed my heart. Seeing my dark-skinned mother Judith's overflowing emotions as me, a man with light skin wept in love and anointed her feet—when she had herself suffered prejudice and hurt—opened my eyes to her profound pain. Healing love is needed! I realized how, as God's children, we are called to be instruments of peace, and that includes emotional healing. God needs us, His body, to be His literal hands and voice of love to others. I asked the Lord to use me in the area of racial and ethnic healing.

Rooming with Angels

By the end of the week, I felt as if I had three angels as roommates. Hebrews 13:2 reminds us, *do not forget to entertain strangers, for by doing so some people have entertained angels without knowing it.* When we follow God's call, we can expect the unexpected, maybe angels! Thankfully, He didn't command me to eat locusts or walk around naked for years. He did, however, ask me to open my door to a stranger, a woman and her son, and through that, I was greatly blessed. Biblical Elijah had a somewhat similar event occur when God commanded him to go to a foreign land and to stay with a woman and her son. Miracles happened for Elijah then, and in our little apartment miracles happened this week. As you just follow, expect the unexpected!

A few weeks later, I received a picture of Judith in a beautiful royal white dress, flowers in her hair, with a formal background with flags and a red wall, like she was being crowned a royal princess. I was in awe; this was how I had seen her when praying! She had been formally recognized by the Government of the Bahamas for her lifetime of service and support. Her face beamed in that picture, radiating all the beautiful love of Christ. My spiritual mother Judith had written this in my journal:

> *Craig, meeting you is like meeting Jesus. You are the salt of the earth, light in this dark world. Let your light continue to shine. There is a soul winner's crown waiting for you. Judith.*

I am blessed beyond anything I could have ever asked for or imagined, just by following Him.

Chapter 9

Few People Change the World (Day 4)

Few people change the world. 😞

Few people change the world. 😊

It all depends on how you look at it!

Sunday evening marked the kickoff of the large Lausanne Conference in South Korea, with over 5,000 people from over 180 nations. There were some delays with the shuttle bus from the hotel to the conference center. God orchestrated this as it gave me the opportunity to meet new people as we waited. One of them was Nadja, who is from Brazil. This allowed me to practice my Portuguese and to hear her amazing story. Nadja runs a home that serves 40 young mothers and their 70 children. We spent a significant amount of time discussing her calling and the struggles these young women face. I shared how I felt called to bless and minister to women, and she was encouraged. She even prayed for me, asking God to raise up more men with a similar calling, as there is a strong need for men to step into this role. Later, Nadja texted me: *Hello, my brother. I haven't seen you since our providential conversation, but my heart is filled with gratitude knowing that God is stirring His male children to look upon the vulnerable women of the world with deep love, compassion, and the restoration of dignity.* Amen! Lord, please call more men to this mission!

The Lausanne Conference opened with an incredible light show and a Hollywood-style production, with a single huge video screen spanning the entire front of the room. This is not my style of worship, but I could greatly appreciate the high levels of work that was invested, excellent quality and professionalism that was on display.

That evening, many inspiring statements were shared, but the one that resonated most with me was made by Michael Oh, the CEO of the Lausanne Committee:

Few people change the world.

This statement can be taken either negatively or positively, depending on how it's said. I chose to hear it positively. A person like me *can* change the world! *You* can change the world! The speaker went on to share that it's not about what we bring, but who we place it in the hands of. He referenced the Bible story of Jesus multiplying five loaves and two fish to feed over 5,000 people. Given there were almost exactly 5,000 people in that huge room, the size of the miracle took on new meaning. I often feel like I didn't even have five loaves or two fish to give, but the little I do have, I want to place in His hands.

Many Streams make One River

Another speaker, Billy Wilson from Empower21, who is also the President of Oral Roberts University, shared a powerful thought: *Many streams make one river.* This resonated with me, as the Bible teaches that Jesus' followers are parts of one body, with Christ as the head. Billy went on to discuss the early church's growth and the lessons we can learn from them: they had conviction, flexibility, obedience to the Holy Spirit, and they broke cultural norms and protocols. They depended on God to provide for their needs and were united in purpose. Unfortunately, as I look at the global church of 2.4 billion believers today, I don't see much of this unity or the other traits that defined the early church. It was refreshing to hear this message and reflect on how much we need to make changes if we expect better results — telling the world of the love of Christ, fulfilling the Great Commission. The call to break protocol and follow the Holy Spirit's guidance spoke directly to me, as it aligns with how I've felt led throughout my own journey. To get the desired impact of love in the world, we have to do things differently!

At the conference, there were over 5,000 people gathered sitting at close to 1,000 tables, the size was overwhelming, but as I soon saw, God's hand was still in the details. We were randomly assigned to tables, and on my right, I had the privilege of sitting next to Stan, the CEO of the *Come and See Foundation*, the distribution arm behind the popular series *The Chosen*. I was thrilled, as my family and I love *The Chosen*, and it was amazing to spend the week getting to know Stan better.

Truly, God blesses us in ways we never expect.

Chapter 10

KNOW Him

Jesus replied…
Though you do not know Him, I know Him.
JOHN 8: 54-55

Her eyes widened as she listened, as we all sat in the college cafeteria. A friend of our youngest son, she had been listening as I had shared a few stories about my experiences — travel, constant prayer, and the adventures of following God. She had often heard me say, *I heard God*, or *I felt God nudge me to…* suddenly she jumped in asking, *How do you hear God?*

It's a question I've been asked many times, and I sure have no monopoly on this! The truth is, anyone can hear God and be guided by Him, it simply starts with knowing Him.

To *follow* you must hear
To *hear* you must trust
To *trust* you must
know God

So, it all starts with knowing God.
Do you KNOW God?

How well do you know Him? Do you trust that He really loves you, even though you have a hard life? How familiar are you with His voice? Can you discern what He is saying from the noise of the world around you?

It is just like a human relationship. If I desire to follow you, I have to know you. Yet there are steps building up to this. When you know a person, you decide if you can trust them. If you trust them, you will listen to them. If you can hear, you can then and only then follow. I have seen where often the most critical step is not the following or hearing, it is the trusting. Can I trust the person? Do they truly desire what is best for me, and do they know the best way to achieve it?

Do I, do you, trust God?

That is the foundational question. To trust Him fully, you need to get to know Him, spending time with Him and study Him. There is no other way to develop trust.

Knowing is Relational

In knowing God, the question is not related only to how well you know the Bible, theology, or the facts about God, Jesus, or the Christian faith. The devil also knows all of that quite well. The leaders who hated and crucified Jesus also knew all of the scripture and theology well. They failed to know God though, to hear His voice, or have his heart of love.

Knowledge is not the same as knowing God.

As Jesus said to the religious leaders in John 5:38-40:
You have never heard his voice nor seen his form, nor does his word dwell in you, for you do not believe the one he sent. You study the Scriptures diligently because you think that in them you have eternal life. These are the very Scriptures that testify about me, yet you refuse to come to me to have life…
You do not have the love of God in your hearts.

A simple test, to know if you know God. Do you love others deeply? This is the natural fruit of a tree that knows God. The leaders Jesus was talking to did not love people, instead loving the rules and knowledge. The Bible tells us this, *Whoever does not love, does not know God, for God is love. (1 John 4:8).*

**The level you love others
shows the level you know God**

Please do not think that God no longer talks or engages personally with you, as I have heard some say. That is absolutely not what the Bible states. God is talking and His followers are hearing, from the first to the last chapter of the Bible. Beginning when God is speaking to Adam and Eve,

Be fruitful and multiply...
GENESIS 1:28

To the very end of the Bible speaking to His followers,
"Come!" and let him who hears say, "Come!"
Whoever is thirsty, let him come and; whoever wishes,
let him take the free gift of the water of life.
REVELATION 22:17

God talks; do you hear Him? He wants you to! So, how can a finite, fragile, earthly being come to *know* the infinite, all-powerful Creator of the universe? It's possible. I know Him, and many others do as well.

If you want to grow a tree, you must first plant a seed. That seed requires attention, discipline, time, and patience (the hardest part for me!). Knowing God requires the same things.

Knowing is very Intimate and Takes Time

In the Old Testament, the word *know* is often used to describe the intimate physical relationship between a husband and wife, *Adam knew Eve and she conceived and bore a son*. To truly know someone is to be very close, open, trusting and vulnerable. This is the kind of relationship God desires with us — a relationship of intimacy. Only when we know Him in this way can we truly trust, hear and follow Him. I like to look at it as a dance with God. It takes time to know how to dance, and to follow His leading!

This book is about the wonder and glory of following God. The foundation — the seed — is intimately knowing Him. If you start there, the fruit of that will naturally be a desire to follow Him with glorious loving fruit nourishing the lives of others.

For me, the process of knowing God has taken years, and my relationship with Him is constantly growing. This will continue for eternity, as fully knowing God is knowing all things, and that is a lot! We start here on earth, and it continues in heaven forever. We will never reach the limits of knowing all of God. Let's get going, there is a lot to know! For me the most important way to know God is my alone time with Him. Over the years, the amount of time I've spent with God has increased. It's like training for a sport: if you spend five minutes a day, you'll see some results. Yet if you spend three hours a day, you'll see a far greater transformation. The more time you invest, the closer your relationship becomes. Think of any human relationship — the more time you spend with someone, the better you get to know them.

Martin Luther, the father of the Protestant Reformation, famously said in the 16th century:

I have so much to do
that I shall have to spend the first three hours in prayer.

Spending time with God is mandatory; it's the necessary training for living a life that ultimately follows Him.

There are countless books written on this subject, so I will just speak of my own personal experience.

How I Get to Know God

Daily Time with God:
I start each day by spending time alone with God every morning. I find mornings easier to control and schedule than evenings, and since I'm a morning person, it works out well.

Reading the Bible:
I take time to read the Bible and meditate on it. As I once told a friend, it's more about quality than quantity. While reading large sections has its place for understanding the bigger picture, God's focus isn't on how quickly we read the Bible, or if we read it all annually, but on how much it transforms us to be more like Jesus.

Listening to God:

This is a newer habit for me. It's a form of meditation where I simply listen for God's voice, and do not talk. I learned this practice from a friend who grew up in a war-torn region of the Middle East and found healing in these quiet moments with God. Over time, I've come to hear God speaking during these times of stillness.

Journaling:

Journaling has become a meaningful way to process my thoughts and see how God is working in my life. I started small, writing occasionally, but over time it's become a regular practice that improves my relationship with God. I highly recommend starting a journal — it's both fun and spiritually enriching.

Staying Attuned to God's Presence:

The Bible tells us that God is always with us *(Deuteronomy 31:6)*. So, I make an effort to stay aware of His presence throughout the day. I talk to Him as I go about my day — praying for people I pass, thanking Him for beauty I see, or asking for guidance before meetings. This keeps me connected to Him and ready to respond to His leading.

Moving On from Mistakes:

We all make mistakes, even big ones. Take comfort, to God they are all the same size! Don't dwell on them. Confess, learn, and move on. Your mistakes do not surprise Him, God knew you're not perfect, prior to receiving you as His child. Like any loving father, He forgives and moves forward with you. If you struggle with a recurring issue, make a plan to address it, just don't let it keep you stuck. God has chosen you, *nothing* can separate you from His love, nothing. So, act like His beloved child, get up and move forward.

Learn from Others:

You're not the first person to follow Jesus! There are centuries of wisdom from those who have walked this path before. Explore writings not only from today's authors but also from Christians who lived hundreds of years ago. With the internet, you can access free versions of these older texts. I didn't read much prior, but these last two years I have read extensively, a few I really enjoyed:

- *Interior Castle* by Teresa of Avila – Nun, 500 years ago, intimacy with Christ. This is a profound book.
- *Diary of St. Faustyna* by Maria Faustyna Kowalska – Nun that lived in Krakow, Poland 100 years ago, died young, intimate diary of relationship with God.
- *Living Flame of Love Commentary* by St John of the Cross – Monk from 500 years ago, intimate poem about God. Amazing depth of close love with God.
- *With Christ in the School of Prayer* by Andrew Murray – Written over 100 years ago, excellent book on prayer, covers everything.
- *Absolute Surrender* by Andrew Murray – a sermon, 1895, truly excellent, and he has other amazing sermons
- *Not Knowing Where* by Oswald Chambers – early 20th century, profound look at the mystery of following God, writer of the famous devotional *My Utmost for His Highest.*
- *The Cost of Discipleship* by Dietrich Bonhoeffer – Written 1930s, Dietrich was a theologian, pastor, and attempted to assassinate Hitler, died by hanging at Hitler's order.
- *The Normal Christian Life* by Watchman Nee – Amazing classic of the Christian faith, Chinese Pastor, died in a prison camp in 1972. Challenges us to live like Jesus.
- *Let Us Pray* by Watchman Nee – On Prayer! Quick read, powerful book. God partnering with man, through prayer.
- *Celebration of Discipline* by Richard Foster – Written 1970s, covering basic foundational disciplines like prayer, fasting, meditation, confession and more.
- *Reese Howell: Intercessor* by Norman Grubb – prayer warrior that lived early 20th Century in England – his prayers influenced WWII, also was a missionary in Africa.
- *Evangelii Gaudium (The Joy of the Gospel)* by Pope Francis, all Protestants have to read this. You should not comment on the Catholic church unless you know the heart of its leader. It is an easy read, free if you download the pdf.

- *Turning Points* by Mark Noll – summary of 2,000 years of church history, must read for every follower of Christ. The Church has been beautiful, but also ugly, we need to know history to not repeat it.
- *Kneeling Christian* by an Unknown Author – likely the best book on prayer I have ever read. Written early 20th Century.
- *The Starfish and the Spirit* by Lance Ford and Rob Wegner – looking at the early church, how was it governed and how it so quickly reproduced and changed the world.
- *My Life in God* by Dominic Sultana – Catholic Priest from Malta, travels extensively, teaching on how to hear God, and writes many amazing books.
- *Draw the Circle* by Mark Batterson – author of many books, this book on prayer changed my life.

These books have inspired me. As you can see, they are from all slices and times of the Christian community and traditions. You are incomplete without them. These are divinely inspired thinkers, learn from others that have gone before you.

Prayer Using the A.C.T.S. Method:

Adoration: Praising God for His attributes — His love, wisdom, joy and more! Who He is.

Confession: Asking God to forgive my mistakes from the previous day. This keeps me close to Him, as sin creates a barrier between us.

Thanksgiving: I go all out here, thanking God for everything — my coffee, family, car, games, health, the couch, pillow, and even the little things like a good book or a fun game. Did I mention coffee? The Bible says, *The joy of the Lord is our strength (Nehemiah 8:10),* and gratitude builds that joy.

Supplication: Praying for others and for myself, asking God to move. As you grow in Christ, you learn to pray not just for what you think is best, but for God's will in each situation. Sometimes He uses challenges to shape us, so it's wise to ask God how He wants you to pray for someone. Are all my prayers always answered like I request? No, of course not. Like a small child, I will ask for things that are not aligned with what God desires. His ways are truly a mystery quite often! I write down key requests in my journal, so have thousands written down, and the vast majority of them have been answered as prayed. With time, as I know Him more, I pray in more alignment with His will. It takes time to know God, He is big!

How much time should I spend with God?

People will ask, *how much time do you spend with God?* I don't like to answer that directly. The reason is that the moment I do, people tend to compare. I like to ask the person; *how much do you want to know God?* What I can say is that there is a clear correlation between the amount of time I spend with God and the number of adventures, joy and purpose I experience. The more time I spend with God, the more incredible things happen. Less time means fewer amazing events and less joy. It's as simple as that—I want to partner with God for more of those amazing experiences, as it makes for the best life. Nothing is better than walking with God!

That said, even as I write this, I can think of times when I failed to prioritize time with Him or have made mistakes, sinning, and not following Him. Yet, God still works wonders through me. He's not limited by my failures. He can still use and bless me. Even so, God doesn't want us to coast. Like in any relationship, if I drift away from spending time with Him, my ability to hear His voice or follow His guidance diminishes. In those times, when I feel distant or unworthy, God uses me in ways that remind me that it's not because of my righteousness that He chooses to use me. It's because of His love for me.

Ask God for Help

Years ago, I knew God wanted me to wake up at 5:30 every morning to spend time with Him. Day after day, week after week, I struggled to get up. I was simply too tired. Finally, in frustration, I cried out, *God! I know you want me to get up at 5:30AM, but I just can't do it. I give up. I'm not going to try anymore.* The very next morning, without setting an alarm, I woke up at

5:30AM. The next day, the same thing happened. God often uses moments like this to show us that our human strength isn't what He's after. He wants us to realize that we are fully dependent on Him to accomplish anything of true value. Let me repeat that:

God wants us to recognize our complete dependence on Him
to do anything of value.

It's natural to think that if God gives us a command, we must carry it out using our own strength. That is not the best way at all! How does our strength compare to the strength of God? The truth is, we can do nothing on our own. We are as helpless as a newborn baby. Jesus said in John 15:5, *apart from me, you can do nothing.* Let that sink in. Without God, we are 100% inadequate to do anything of value. We can without God easily make a mess of things, that is about all we can do! We must remain in Him. As Jesus says in John 15:4,

No branch can bear fruit by itself; it must remain in the vine.
Neither can you bear fruit unless you remain in me.

Knowing God is your Foundation.

There is nothing better than knowing Him. Your path may be similar to mine, but it will not be identical. He will likely keep changing your routine, keeping you dependent on following Him, so don't get too comfortable!

You need a strong foundation, that requires knowing God well. Without it, your life will look like the *Leaning Tower of Pisa* in Italy!

Raymond, an expert architect, whose company designed many Walmart stores globally, told me this:

The most important part to any building is its foundation.
Don't rush it, build it right, invest in it.

Do not fall over.
Invest in your foundation. KNOW Him well.

Chapter 11

Pray and Obey
(Day 5)

The prayer of a righteous man
is powerful and effective.
Elijah was a man just like us.
He prayed earnestly that it would not rain
and it did not rain on the land for 3 ½ years
JAMES 5:16-17

Elijah was just like us, and his prayers changed the weather. Do you believe this? Do your actions reflect that belief?

It was Monday, the first full day of the conference. I left my hotel before 6 AM and took a taxi to arrive early enough to pray again in the Workplace track room. On the way there, I received a text from my friend, a Korean woman in our small prayer group back in the U.S. She had felt led by God to send me 2 Chronicles 7:1-3, a verse she believed was meant for me and the conference. When I read it in the taxi, I was stunned — it was exactly what I would end up praying just minutes later on the stage in prayer for the day! Arriving there at the facility, I prayed through 2 Chronicles 6:41-42 and 2 Chronicles 7:1-3, parts of it are: *Now, arise, O Lord God, and come to your resting place... When Solomon finished praying, fire came down from heaven and consumed the burnt offering and the sacrifices, and the glory of the Lord filled the temple.* It was pure joy walking through the huge room where 1,500 people would be sitting. Then praying at the podium, asking for God's glory to fill the space, for His fire to come down and rest in the room. It was a powerful time, and I felt led to pray that God would heal many wounded hearts in this room. He heard. He would. I would be blessed to be used to heal in His name.

The vast room was warm, and as I walked alone, I had to shed my dress shirt, praying in just my white t-shirt. Only later did I learn that the AC was turned on at 8 AM! Even though I was hot, uncomfortable, and alone, I felt the presence of God in that time of prayer. It was marvelous. I've heard people say that location doesn't matter when you pray, and there's truth in that. However, there are also many instances in the Bible where God commanded His people to pray in specific places. I have experienced it myself, where obedience to God's call to a particular location has led to miracles. Following God's direction is key, even when others might not understand. That morning, in that massive hot room as I walked it alone, I felt God's glory descend, and it set the tone for the week ahead. Maybe the room was warm due to the fire of God descending!

The whole group of almost 50 workplace speakers and volunteers were invited to the morning prayer time. At 8 AM, two joined for prayer: Charles from Singapore and Vivek from India. It was interesting though, as the first thing they did, was talk about U.S. politics. Particularly the significance of the state of Arizona, where I live, in upcoming elections and how government and business should work together. Charles' comments about the U.S. being the light of the world struck me as further confirmation from the Lord that He will be leading me toward a role in the U.S. Government.

Freedom in Christ

The main conference session was in a different area from the workplace conference hall, so I made my way there. During a break, in this huge crowd, I was amazed to run into a pastor from the U.S. Not sure how or why, but he shared that he avoided talking to women alone at conferences, like this one, to avoid what others may think. It was an unusual talk given we had not seen each other in over a year. There was a tangible spirit of fear in his words. As I left that brief talk, I was wondering why that had occurred, as I tried to race to the restroom during the break. God highlighted a man as I walked and I knew I needed to stop and talk to him. Maybe it was how he was dressed, from top to bottom in an African-style light blue outfit, almost like a robe. He was a pastor from Ghana I learned. He shared how the session had meant a lot to him, and how he had learned personally to obey the Holy Spirit, telling me,

If the Holy Spirit says, 'Do it,' you do it!

I asked if I could pray for him, and I was blessed to pray for this new brother, and quickly I turned to finally make it to the bathroom.

Passing the Test

As he walked off, I pivoted and immediately saw a young woman in a wheelchair at a table right in front of me. The Holy Spirit immediately nudged me to pray for her and to pray for healing. My mind immediately flashed to the advice from the U.S. pastor about avoiding interactions with women, and how I still had not made it to the restroom. Yet the voice of the Holy Spirit was very clear: *Do it!*, and with that command, the words of the pastor from Ghana flooded my mind. Oh, how the enemy likes to plant seeds of fear, how God instructs us, then there is the test of who I will listen to – the enemy or God. It would just become more amazing as I chose to follow God, walking over to her. Kneeling down next to her, I learned her name is Visola from Madagascar. As we spoke, I told her that I knew one person from Madagascar and her name was Mandisa, one of the speakers for the workplace track who I had worked with for months. Visola's eyes grew wide, I didn't know what was going on. Then, a sudden huge smile broke from ear to ear. She told me how she had traveled with my friend Mandisa, who was a dear friend of hers. Mandisa had told her all about an American man that prayed for her in a wonderful way. *Wow, word travels fast,* I thought! Visola was hoping to meet that man, and I had just walked over to her in a room with 5,000 people in it. I asked if I could pray for her leg, and with excitement she asked me to pray. As I placed my hands on the cast on her leg, I could sense God's love and presence. I prayed for physical healing, and that she would feel God's great love for her as His daughter. I was just in awe. The enemy had moved, but God had checkmated him as I followed God's leading. Having pushed through the fear, victory always feels good! Following the Holy Spirit brings blessings to others.

How do you Succeed?

In the main session, the speaker shared a story about Pastor Cho, who founded the Yoido Full Gospel Church, the largest megachurch in the world. When Pastor Cho was asked how the church grew so large, he responded with two simple words:

Pray and Obey

I couldn't agree more. That was my morning, learning how to do that, and it wasn't even lunchtime yet!

Humility Comes Before Honor

In the afternoon, the workplace track began. Our team of volunteers scrambled to prepare, and I asked the leader if we could start with prayer. Joseph, the overall leader, looked at me and said, *Great idea! Why don't you do it!* I was humbled and honored to lead the kickoff in prayer for the gathering of 1,500 leaders from over 120 nations. The time spent that morning in prayer and walking the room was reaping a huge harvest. God's Spirit filled the room with excitement. The session went smoothly, and I had the privilege of praying with the speakers individually, prior to them walking up on the stage and speaking, it felt like we were on a common mission together.

Wisdom's instruction is to fear the Lord,
and humility comes before honor.
PROVERBS 15:33

Islam and the Love of God

That afternoon, I attended a session on Islam and the Muslim world. There, I met Vicky, a man from Pakistan, and learned about his work running a school for 270 girls in Afghanistan who were denied access to education. He shared that for just $10,000 a year, they could educate 300 more girls. This moved me, especially after a conversation with a family I know in the

USA. They are Afghan refugees, and I had talked at length with the father, as part of his family is still back in Afghanistan, with greatly restricted freedom. All of this reinforced how we as Jesus followers need to act like a united Body, transferring finances to places that need it most. The Courageous Third platform God was calling me toward would enable this.

God's timing is amazing. In the middle of this session about the Muslim world, Dulce, a missionary from Brazil who lives in Jordan, received a concerning message from her husband in Jordan. Their house church had been discovered by the police. We all gathered around her, holding hands, and prayed for God's protection for her family. It was another beautiful example of how the body of Christ is needed and how we need to work together.

Pray and Obey
Yes, it is that simple.

Chapter 12

Seeing the One
(Day 6)

If a man owns a hundred sheep,
and one of them wanders away,
will he not leave the ninety-nine on the hills
and go to look for the one that wandered off?
MATTHEW 18:12

On the bus ride in, I was blessed to sit next to a pastor from Kenya. Coincidentally, he had been married almost exactly the same length of time as I have, so we instantly had something in common. Years ago, he felt called by God to serve single young women with children. This resonated with me because I too felt called to minister to women. For the hour-long ride to the conference, he shared what he has learned over the years. He emphasized how the Bible instructs us to care for the most vulnerable, often women and especially those with children. He explained that women need jobs to regain a sense of value and worth, especially when they've been hurt. The Pastor referenced Elijah living with the widow and her son. Elijah showing her love and care by meeting her needs, as she worked cooking and taking care of him, it was a job that gave her tangible worth.

Two Wombs

The pastor spoke about how, when women are wounded by men, their hearts often grow cold. This is particularly common when they feel crushed and lose pride, which can happen when they lack work. He pointed out that in the Bible, the word *father* is reserved for only God and man. Being a father carries the responsibility of creating, sustaining, and protecting life. Women, he said, have two wombs: a physical one for bearing children and an emotional one for nurturing. When a woman's heart is hurt, her recovery takes longer than a man because God designed her to feel deeply. A wounded heart requires protection and agape love. Agape love is divine love, where it is fully focused on caring for the other and meeting their needs.

The pastor also shared how he saw that the modern feminist concept that *men are not needed* actually harms women. Emphasizing that real men should embody love and protection, lifting a woman up. He sharing how every woman he has met longs for a real man, full of this agape love. When women have been hurt though, they have closed that door, as their hearts have been wounded. By the end of the hour, I was amazed. I had gained more insight into this subject than I ever had prior, and it reaffirmed my calling to empower and uplift women in line with God's intentions.

Is God Worth more than Everything?

I missed the start of the conference session because I was having a meaningful conversation with my friend Jack. We talked and prayed together in the large workplace conference hall, as he's been facing family issues, especially between his daughter and son-in-law. Jack shared how Philippians 3:8 has been a comfort to him: *What is more, I consider everything a loss compared to the surpassing greatness of knowing Christ Jesus my Lord, for whose sake I have lost all things. I consider them rubbish, that I may gain Christ.*

With tears in his eyes, Jack explained how he's learning that God alone is enough, even when it feels like so much has been taken away. He compared himself to Joseph, who was imprisoned to learn humility, before God used him to save many. Jack spoke about how he has centered his life on God, leaving the outcomes in His hands. His realization that *being with God IS the promised land* was beautiful. It challenged me to ask myself if God alone is enough to satisfy me. God perfectly orchestrated the timing to hear this, as God would open my eyes a few days later. In talking to Jack, God had planted the seed for me to slowly realize that I truly only wanted to just follow Him.

What is the Worth of Woman?

Later, I discovered it was ethnic dress-up day at the conference. In the hall, I met four women dressed in exotic traditional silk dresses, looking like Disney princesses! I asked for a picture with them. Laughing, they agreed, as I stood there in the middle. They joked about how I was bringing Pakistan and India together, as the women were from those countries, which historically do not get along. One woman, Jaganmata from India, stood out to me. Over lunch, we connected as she shared her background in the professional business world, having worked for Abbott Labs — a background I could relate to. I prayed for her, and she told me, *I feel seen and valued. Thank you for this gift.* I praised God for guiding me to her. I pondered how just spending undivided time with her, listening, and praying had meant so much to her. This simple act showed her she had value.

At dinner, I talked with another Indian woman, Mabella. God had highlighted her during a video prayer call a month prior. She is a senior government employee and the recipient of a prestigious state award this year. As we spoke, she shared about her upbringing as one of six daughters in a family, with the youngest child being a boy. I must have widened my eyes, as she read my mind, saying, *My parents kept trying for a boy, no woman ever prays for a daughter.* This pierced my heart. She explained the cultural bias in this majority Christian part of India, and how it left her feeling as a second-class citizen, due simply to being a woman. The pain was still there, in a grown woman, that is a wife with two children of her own in high school. Once again, I was confronted with the painful reality that cultures, even Christian cultures, can diminish women's value, crushing them in the process. The Bible calls us to do the opposite, uplifting and healing, defending and supporting.

A father to the fatherless, a defender of the widows, is God in his holy dwelling. God sets the lonely in families...
PSALM 68:5-6

I cried out to God as she kept talking, asking why He kept showing me this pain women have, and He answered: *So, you can feel their pain and show merciful love.* After hearing her story, we prayed for each other, and she blessed me with her prayer, *God, give Craig the nations and the desires of his heart. God bless his ministry to women.*

Seeing the One

As I was late to hear the conference speaker, I was walking quickly to the main hall. An older man tripped over his suitcase and fell tumbling to the floor. Helping him up I met retired Professor Pramod, who had just arrived at the conference from India. He was exhausted, struggling with his luggage, and needed help. Skipping part of the evening session, we shared dinner, and as we talked, he told me how in every classroom he taught he prayed to *see the one* — the student who truly needed his help. His words struck me.

The most important thing in life is to see the one,
because that's who God cares for.

My natural tendency is to think in large numbers, as I did in my corporate career, where in Corporate Finance I managed the software responsible for the multi-billion-dollar financials at Intel. Over the years, God has been focusing me on the one, teaching me to care about individuals, as people are God's highest priority. God knows each person by name, intimately. Pramod's wisdom reinforced that lesson: love is best given one person at a time.

At the conference, at our table I was blessed to talk with Kevin from Uganda. Kevin shared his feelings of being judged because his church is smaller than others. I prayed for him, his family, and his ministry. Afterward, he told me that this short prayer time with me was the highlight of the conference. He encouraged me to meet his friend Grace, who runs coffee shops, so I could pray for her as well. I was able to meet with Grace later in the week, and had a wonderful time listening to her and blessing her in prayer. She had arrived to talk with me overwhelmed with work stress, and left smiling with renewed trust that God would guide her through the fog of running a small company in multiple countries.

As the day was wrapping up, I was helping Professor Pramod check into the hotel and get to his room. I reflected on what he said. To *see the one* reminded me that God's love is meant to reach individuals in a personal way, as that is how He sees everyone.

See the One. God does.
He lovingly pursues the one sheep.
May we see, then do the same.

If a man owns a hundred sheep,
and one of them wanders away,
will he not leave the ninety-nine on the hills
and go to look for the one that wandered off?
MATTHEW 18:12

Chapter 13

You Need Others

Therefore, since we are surrounded
by such a great cloud of witnesses
HEBREWS 12:1

These 40 days would not have happened without Raymond.

I met Raymond a year ago at a house party hosted by a mutual friend, Bruce, who leads the Merrill-Lynch Christian Employee group. During the event, we had a brief introduction, and Raymond was specifically highlighted by God to me, as someone I should talk to. I have learned to follow those promptings when God highlights someone—it's always for a reason. I felt a bit awkward approaching him, as Raymond is a senior leader, well-connected, globally experienced, and highly intelligent. As the evening wore on and the guests began to leave, we found ourselves alone, standing by the fireplace, and we started talking. I was blessed to hear his heart, about travels to Africa, failures, and his desire to follow Christ in every small detail of life. It was inspiring. Raymond has since become a role model to me, someone I greatly admire—he's about 15 years older than me, and I truly look up to him. We all need people like that in our lives.

Over time, Raymond and I would connect a few times each month. He generously shared his life with me—his joys, struggles, current circumstances, and the lessons he was learning from God. It's rare to find someone so open, and Raymond's willingness to open his heart to me was the greatest gift he could give. His authenticity and love for others are powerful examples of what God calls us to. Raymond exemplified this kind of open book life in his own walk with Christ. One key concept he shared with me has stayed with me:

I feel my time on Earth is short, so I want the veil between my life here and heaven to be as thin as possible. That way, when I enter heaven, there will only be the smallest change, as there I will continue doing the same things I did on Earth.

He reflects on this daily, considering whether to spend his time playing golf or mentoring someone, or whether to hold onto his wealth or give it away.

In May 2024, during a conversation with Raymond, he felt that God was calling me to attend the Lausanne Korea conference in September, to take his place. Raymond sits on the Board of Directors for Lausanne, and had planned to attend the conference, but he is above all a follower of God. He sensed that God was asking him to send me instead, offering me his spot and introduced me to the Lausanne CEO. It was an unexpected and humbling opportunity. Raymond had paid for his ticket which he gave to me. Through his obedience to God, I was able to attend the Lausanne Korea conference and embark on this 40-day journey that created this book and opened doors to pray for hundreds of people.

I did not open the door for this trip – Raymond did.

His close relationship with God allowed him to hear God's voice, and as God's servant, he obeyed. This was an incredible blessing for me, but it was also a blessing for Raymond. God knew that in this period of the conference, Raymond would be needed back in the U.S., where one of his children needed medical treatment and as his mother-in-law passed away.

This journey has reminded me of the importance of walking humbly and recognizing that we are not alone. We are fully dependent on God and others. It is often our dear brothers and sisters in Christ who help open the doors for us.

We run this as a team.

Chapter 14

Blessed Feet
(Day 7)

He poured water into a basin and
began to wash his disciples' feet
JOHN 13:5

Waking up early again on Wednesday, I took a taxi to the conference center to pray. While waiting for the taxi, met a European woman who was clearly attending the convention. During our conversation, she suddenly told me she felt I had to meet a man she had just spoken to — Scott from Sweden. I took his contact information as I jumped into the taxi, once again wondering what God was orchestrating.

When I arrived early at the conference center, it was as empty as usual at that hour. I had the privilege of spending hours in prayer, reading the Bible, and walking around the workplace room. Again, praying for God to fill the room with His love and insight for attendees. I started to feel hungry; breakfast was needed prior to the main session starting. I began walking toward the closest door near the main stage, but all the way in the back of the room, I noticed a woman sitting at a table her head down, either praying or crying. God whispered to me, *Don't eat now. Go talk to her.* So, as my stomach growled, I walked across the large room and realized it was Yatima from Africa, one of our speakers. Her face lit up with a huge smile when I sat next to her.

She told me she had wanted to talk and pray with me the day before, but had felt discouraged because I was busy talking and praying with Jack. Now, she felt God had answered her prayers as I had walked directly over to her right at that moment. We talked and she shared her fears about speaking in front of 1,500 people. As we sat in the room where she would soon be speaking, I was blessed to pray for her. As I prayed, God led me to kneel and to pray specifically over her feet. She was moved, tears filling her eyes. She felt seen, loved, and ready to speak at the conference. I was incredibly blessed by the encounter, once again in awe of how God moves when we follow His lead.

Run to the Darkness

Afterward, I raced downstairs to grab breakfast, stopping at a convenience store for chocolate and yogurt. While eating at a table in the hallway, I struck up a conversation with Kamal from Lebanon. He explained the complex political situation in his country, where power is shared between three religious groups. For years, the Christian part of the government, which fills the presidency, has been without a president due to ongoing disputes. His story touched me, especially since a friend of mine in Lebanon had been sending me pictures of the destruction and ongoing unrest in the war. We prayed for Lebanon and the region, and it reminded me that, as followers of Jesus, we are called to engage with the struggles of the world, not turn away from them. I recently heard a religious leader say, *politics is the devil's playground, and believers should not go into it.* While there may be some truth in that, it's precisely why we should step into the darkness and bring His light.

Wherever it is darkest is where light is most needed.
Go there.

A *comfortable cowardly* view, is unacceptable for a follower of God. Do not run from darkness in fear, God has given you the keys of heaven, his power. Light up the darkness! Jesus said:

I will build my church, and the gates of hell will not
overcome it. I will give you the keys of the kingdom of
heaven; whatever you bind on earth will be bound in heaven,
and whatever you loose on earth will be loosed in heaven.
MATTHEW 16: 18-19

People feel God's Love and Power as we Follow

After the quick breakfast, I was running late but stopped to grab a coffee from the cafeteria, because life is better with coffee! As I walked by a group, I overheard a woman being interviewed, I heard nothing but one word *marketplace*, and that stopped me. The Holy Spirit nudged me to listen. After she finished, I introduced myself, with the man who had been interviewing her at her side. Her name is Darla, from Canada, where she runs a ministry for women skateboarders. As we stood there by the coffee, I asked if I could pray for her. She immediately closed her eyes and put out her hands as if to receive a gift. While praying, I felt led to kneel on the concrete floor of the cafeteria, praying for physical protection of her feet, sensing God's desire to protect her in her ministry. Also, for her to sense how pleased God is with her loving and serving these young women. When I finished, she stepped back with wide eyes and a shocked look, which surprised me. She thanked me saying, *You have a gift, but I feel like you don't realize it.* Her words reminded me of a similar experience earlier in the year in Poland, talking to two young Ukrainian refugees for over an hour telling them about the love of Jesus. I had finished by praying for them, one then saying, *You have a power.* It has to be God of course; I am just reflecting Him! I hear my own prayers, they are just normal words that come out of my mouth. However, I witness the impact of prayer — people feel seen, loved, and blessed, their life is changed. God moves when we pray over someone, as it penetrates deep into their heart and they feel the tender life-giving love of God. It may be prayer for a brother or sister in Christ, or an Atheist, Sikh, Jew, Muslim, Hindu, Baha'i or anyone. Their background or even religious beliefs don't matter - they are blessed and overwhelmed with thanks. The stories of prayer I could tell, for an atheist leader outside of Moscow, for an Iranian Muslim friend, a Jewish friend, a Sikh buddy, and so many others. It is just amazing, fully God as He partners with us to bless! We get to be the conduit; it is God they sense and His overwhelming love for them. When we follow God, we are His ambassadors, and as such, others see who we represent, God, with all of His love and power to heal.

To God, The One is the Priority

After the workplace track finished for the day, I was excited to talk with one of the speakers, Henry, who is the founder of Faith Driven Investor. I had a chance to pray with him earlier, as I was doing with all the speakers. He was interested to hear more about what God had called me to. Yet, as I waited to talk to him, I felt God directing me to speak with a man who had been staring at me from a few tables away. I walked to him. Soon Russ, a pastor from Indonesia, and I were in a very personal conversation. He opened up about the challenges in his marriage and family. We wept together as he shared how his wife felt neglected and hurt by his parents' treatment, and how their daughter was suffering due to it all. His eyes wide, tears falling, he talked between tissues that he had never shared this with anyone before. I prayed with him, holding his hands, as we both wept. He expressed how this conversation justified the difficult decision to attend the conference despite opposition from his wife, and with limited finances. He said he felt God had commanded him to go, he was glad he followed. Russ asked if he could video me talking to his wife, to tell her how much he loved her. I did tell her, speaking to his phone as he filmed me. He sent it to her that day. It was a profound moment, in this room where, just a few days before, God had led me to pray that hearts would be healed. It was happening, and I was blessed to be part of it! I was in awe of how God works, and how by simply following God's promptings, I could help my brother in Christ. In wonder at what had just happened, and thankful I had prioritized time with Russ, I started to walk out to the food area and to see if I could still track Henry down to talk to him.

As I prepared to leave, God highlighted a woman from our group, named Julie, who lives in the Caribbean. I felt a clear prompting from God to sit next to her and talk with her. I asked God *what about Henry?* and I felt God just smile and tell me again to sit by Julie.

So, I sat down and asked how she was doing. She began to cry as she shared the financial struggles she was facing back home in her island nation. She spoke of decades of faithful service to God and the pain she felt from a group of male pastors who had promised their support but never followed through. Julie felt abandoned, believing that God no longer loved her or cared for her. I listened, held her, and prayed with her, joining her in tears as she cried out to God for help. Together, we poured our hearts out in prayer, asking for God's blessing on her — for the years of suffering she had endured, the financial burden she carried, and the hurt she felt.

When we finished praying, Julie looked at me with a beautiful, sincere question: *I see you pouring into so many, but who pours into you?* I smiled and replied, *That's a great question. My wife pours into me with beautiful nurturing love, and God places people in my life to talk to. Mostly though, I feel like it's God Himself who pours into me, allowing me to pour out love and care for others.* I was blessed she would care to ask; that was the first time anyone had asked me that. We sat silently there at the table together. Julie from the Caribbean, who called me her little brother while I called her my sister. It was wonderful. We sat in a room filled with hundreds of people, yet it felt like it was just the two of us. Only God could do this.

The Unexpected Gift is the Best Gift

As lunch was nearing its end, I then rushed out to grab some food before the line closed. There, standing alone, was Henry — the very person I had been wanting to talk to all afternoon. I was surprised. Every other time, he had been surrounded by people, but now, he was by himself trying to get some food just like I was. We had a great conversation, exchanged contact information, and agreed to catch up more later. As I sat back down to quickly eat, I was in awe of how when we follow God's leading, He orchestrates everything far better than we ever could.

When we serve, kneeling down, including blessing the feet of others, we are richly blessed. **Walk toward others!**

Chapter 15

The GREAT Path
(Day 7-continued)

Whether you turn to the right or to the left,
your ears will hear a voice behind you, saying,
'This is the way; walk in it'
ISAIAH 30:21

Wednesday night, halfway through the conference. I was exhausted but overflowing with joy. I sensed the Lord urging me to take a taxi back to the hotel early, so I could rest. My roommates, Judith, Peter, and Timothy, had gone to the border between South and North Korea to pray. I was alone, there in the room on the white plastic folding chair, reflecting on all that had happened. The next day marked the seven-year anniversary of a life-changing decision, and I needed space to process.

This trip to Asia had been filled with seeing God at work, especially during personal one-on-one conversations and prayer with people from many nations. For the first time in decades, I felt truly content, knowing I was walking closely with God. I could hear His voice clearly, feel His touch, and follow His lead. This filled me with indescribable joy and contentment. Suddenly, the words of a friend from Canada came to mind — a prayer from over a year ago, quoting Isaiah 30:21:

Whether you turn to the right or to the left, your ears will
hear a voice behind you, saying, 'This is the way; walk in it.'

It was happening. I was hearing God's voice and following. In that moment, God opened my eyes, and I was overwhelmed with joy, like my blind eyes could finally drink in the colors of this new world around me. Filled with emotion, I wrote in my journal:

The GREAT path is walking with Jesus.

It's that simple. Walking with Jesus. Following Him, is the best life ever! It is the GREAT path. I would give up everything else just to maintain this closeness with Him. May you learn this faster than I did, it has taken me years.

Exactly seven years and one day prior, God gave me a massive life choice. Today, in Korea alone in this hotel room, I finally knew I had made the right choice. That realization was that even if none of my plans or God's promises for my life ever came true, I would be content. Walking with Him, knowing Him, filled me fully. I was living that now, and nothing in the world could compare. The words of the Apostle Paul in Philippians 3:8 now made perfect sense:

I consider everything a loss compared to the surpassing
greatness of knowing Christ Jesus my Lord,
for whose sake I have lost all things.
I consider them rubbish, that I may gain Christ.

Nothing this world offers, could compare to this sense of fulfillment I had. Not even the realization of my dreams or the calling I felt God had placed on my life. Nothing was more satisfying than knowing Him, feeling His presence, and walking closely at His side. Being His hands and voice, pouring out His love to others — it was incredible.

I had lost control, but I had gained GREAT.
I was walking with God.

Me, a mortal, weak, failure-prone man, was walking at the side of the loving Creator of all things, sensing Him look at me and smile. I was in awe sitting there on the white plastic folding chair alone in the room.

The Choice: Good or Great?

This life-changing decision that I was reflecting on took place seven years earlier, while I was flying from Arizona to California on a business trip to fire one of my employees — a trip no one ever wants to make. During the flight, while reading the Bible, I felt God speak to me, offering me a choice:

Do you want the GOOD path, or
the GREAT path for your life?

I used to like control. I was a finance controller at the time paid to control things, how God has a sense of humor! On the flight, as I looked out the window at the clouds far below, I spent 30 minutes asking God about the pros and cons of each path so I could make the best decision. Looking back, it's amazing that God didn't strike that jet with lightning! Here I was, questioning the Creator of heaven and earth about how much better *great* was than *good*. When God created the universe, He called it good; He was now offering me great! Yet, with the patience of a loving father talking to his small child, God answered my questions and waited while I deliberated. He made it clear that the good path was indeed very good. At the time, I was on track to become the financial systems controller for Intel Corporation, which had a $80 billion revenue stream — a fantastic career. God said the great path was truly GREAT! However, He made it clear, it would be like the path of Abraham — filled with uncertainty, mystery, pain, and challenges — and also the path of Joseph.

After deliberating at 32,000 feet, I finally chose the great path. The very next day, my career seemed to fall off a cliff, launching me into a seven-year journey of wondering, *What is God doing? How is this the GREAT path?* It was filled with the complexity, frustration, adventure, hurt, and mystery of Abraham as God had promised. The part about the path of Joseph is still unclear to me, but that is also becoming clearer. Joseph the parent of Jesus is known as the *Father of Orphans,* which matches this incredible empathy and acting in a fatherly way toward men and women in need of a father. Also, I reflect on the Joseph in Egypt who was elevated to serve in government. God's promises are true, and it will occur in His timing, as Isaiah 60:22 tells us, *I am the Lord, in its time I will do this swiftly.* Amen!

In Korea, the day before the anniversary, I finally understood:
The GREAT path is just following God

This same offer to follow Him, Jesus gave the apostles. Yet it took me years to fully grasp how great it is to just follow, as I had mistakenly believed that my control would successfully guide me to a fulfilling life. I had been wrong. I had tasted following God, and it is much better. God was incredibly patient, helping me realize that the greatest blessing in life is to simply follow Him, to walk and be in His presence. As 2 Peter 3:9 says, *The Lord is not slow in keeping His promise, as some understand slowness. He is patient with you...* Amen, I am glad!

Will you Follow?

It requires surrendering control to Him. There is a cost. You'll be different from those around you. The path is narrow, and few find it. I encourage you — have courage, ask God for help. Tell Him you desperately want it. This is the path to the best life possible.

There on the 15th floor I wrote in my journal that evening:
The great path is knowing You Lord. Walking with You. Hearing You. Feeling You guide me. Seeing You use me to bless others as they feel Your touch, hear Your voice, and receive Your love. Lord, for the first time in a long time, I feel fully content. Even if the dreams You gave me never come true, even if Your promises never occur, if I never see the fruit of my life, I am content – fully satisfied – because I know You. I feel complete. I am walking beside You, obeying every nudge; this is truly the GREAT path! Knowing You is all I want. Obeying You is all I want. The dreams and passions You Lord have placed in my heart are but rubbish compared to knowing you, feeling your pleasure. I thank You Lord, for changing my heart. I am Yours. This is the great path – walking close to You, my Father.

Then I felt God speak to me:
Now you are ready. You are following well; you love the one.
I can now entrust you with the many.

Wow! I wrote:
Amen, Lord. Thank You. I receive.

Tomorrow was the seven-year anniversary of my decision to walk this great path, and I could hardly sleep. My roommates returned late that night from their adventure at the North Korean border, sharing how they almost accidentally drove into North Korea and were stopped by guards protecting the border. They had prayed at the border and blown a shofar — an ancient ram's horn trumpet used in Israel. Timothy loved blowing the shofar, and he often wanted to blow it out our 15th-floor hotel window at night or early in the morning. I had successfully convinced him not to. It wouldn't have been well-received in quiet, proper South Korea! My roommates from the Bahamas were such a blessing. As I lay on my bed up in the loft, I could hear the other three down below getting ready for bed. I reflected on how I did not have roommates with me, but close family. This truly is great.

The GREAT Path is Just Following God

Chapter 16

Walking with God (Day 8)

Now you are the body of Christ,
and each one of you are a part of it
1 CORINTHIANS 12:27

I woke up with a smile on my face, reflecting on the significance of this day — seven years since I chose to walk the GREAT path. God had shown me that this path was simply about following Him. Walking with Him, is what makes it great.

After praying with my dear family from the Bahamas, I suddenly felt God prompt me, *Leave now!* Unsure why, I quickly put on my shoes and rushed to the elevator. Once inside the crowded elevator, I was amazed to find Jala from Uganda standing right in front of me! I had just received a text saying she was needed for an interview, and I was supposed to find her. There she was, perfectly timed. We spoke and sat together on the bus, marveling at how God works in mysterious ways.

While on the bus, I received a message from Abed, a friend from northern Israel. He sent videos of missiles being intercepted by the Israeli Iron Dome defense system, right above his house. He was worried about his wife and three children, especially since they had just welcomed their third baby the previous month. There I was, in Korea, praying with my sister from Uganda for a friend in Israel. It was a beautiful reminder of how God's love connects His global family as one body.

Divine Connections

I walked into the conference area through a different entrance than usual, which turned out to be exactly where I was supposed to meet Scott from Sweden. I had only gotten his contact info the day before, I didn't even know what he looked like, but everything worked out perfectly for us to grab coffee together. Scott is the leader of Operation Mobilization in Europe, and he's passionate about forming missional communities in workplaces or homes, outside of traditional church settings. His vision is to create a space where people can grow as God's priests and saints, crossing denominational lines. This aligned perfectly with the goals of the Courageous Third program, which aims to develop an AI-driven individualized methodology for spiritual growth. It was incredible how God connected us. Between Scott's Protestant experience and my friend Dominic, who is a Catholic priest from Malta who has worked on spiritual growth AI methodologies for years, we had both major traditions covered. God's timing is always perfect. Now I knew why God had miraculously connected us, through a European lady I had met waiting for a taxi!

It was only 9AM, and already God had orchestrated so much! This anniversary was off to an amazing start.

Gossiping the Gospel: at Work

At the Lausanne Conference, the workplace was the focus for Thursday, September 26th. A speaker from Brazil spoke about how the early church shared the gospel in the workplace, as naturally as breathing. This is why it was not even specifically called out, with the speaker even memorably saying, *the gospel was gossiped.* We are all called to tell others about God's love! The scripture from 1 Peter 2:9 resonated: *But you are a chosen people, a royal priesthood, a holy nation, God's special possession.* Romans 1:7 also reminded us that we are even called saints. Yet, many don't realize this, as I often experience people assuming I am a paid pastor or clergy after I pray for them. Praying for others is what priests and saints are called to do, and that is what each of us Jesus followers are.

That day marked the final session of the workplace track. Over 1,500 people from more than 120 nations were gathered again in the room. Like every other day, I was honored to open the session with prayer. My heart was full of joy, surrounded by so many of God's children. A generous donor provided enough Workplace Study Bibles for everyone in attendance. As I was helping wrap up the session on the stage, I noticed a Japanese woman standing at the very edge of the stage clutching the Bible she had just received, just looking at me. God highlighted her and told me to go speak with her and ask her about her story, even though I was quite busy wrapping up the session. I followed God's nudging, and we left and sat down in the lobby outside. Shiori is a missionary from Japan who had spent a decade helping the poor in Ethiopia. God blessed her beautifully and unexpectedly! As she was in Ethiopia, she met a Japanese man who was now her fiancée. She was busy preparing for their wedding in early 2025. She had given up the dream of marriage years ago and all of this was a beautiful blessing, but also very sudden. She was struggling with her next steps in life, so I listened, then prayed for her and her upcoming marriage. Afterward, she was filled with peace and the love of Christ. Telling me it was the most meaningful moment of the conference for her. I felt blessed to be used by God to share His love and comfort with Shiori. *[Little did either of us know at the time, but immediately after this trip, she was diagnosed with cancer and would spend months in the hospital. My wife and I would continue to pray for her and her husband. Amen, how God works!]*

A Dear African Sister

After this, rushed to meet with Mandisa from Madagascar, who was a speaker at the Workplace track area. She was seeking career advice and struggling with how to care for her aging parents. We needed a quiet place to talk, so I asked God to guide us. I felt prompted to go to the fourth floor, a place I had never been, and God led us very miraculously to a perfect location to meet. Amazing how God provided, as I had never even been in this part of the large building. For the first 30 minutes of talking, we discussed her career, but then I felt the Holy Spirit nudge me to stop and ask about her heart. She hesitated, then broke down in tears, sharing the weight of her responsibilities caring for her parents and the feeling her life was passing by. In that moment, I felt I was sitting next to a daughter of the King. I was blessed to be able to pray for her and to speak words of life, love, and who she is in Christ – His beloved daughter. Mandisa told me she had a sister, but always wished she could have an older brother. Now she felt like she had one, and I saw her as my little sister. God's presence was so tangible, raw uncontainable joy filled me. This moment reminded me of His promise from June 2023, just over a year prior, when I had been at the Dead Sea in Israel. It had been an amazing morning, sitting on a sandy salty peninsula alone with God at sunrise, surrounded by the Dead Sea. God had asked me what I wanted. I was amazed, and felt like it was a Solomon moment, when God had asked him the same question. I requested that God use my life to richly bless others. He responded, saying He would, and that I would be His hands and voice to bless many. God also said that even these two other areas I also desired, but had not asked for, He would give me. It had been a miraculous morning there at the Dead Sea, and I was seeing on this day in Korea over a year later God's promise come to life, again. I had truly been God's hands and voice to bless a daughter of the King, a woman from Madagascar, who I am now blessed to call my sister. Wow!

After the conference, I boarded the bus back to the hotel, feeling exhausted yet grateful. God though wasn't done blessing yet. I sat next to Karishma from India, a digital marketing consultant who had recently left her job, feeling called to something new. We had a great conversation about her journey and how God had been leading me. Sitting on a bench outside the hotel, we prayed together. Karishma even offered me excellent business advice for the Courageous Third project! It made me laugh—here I was, receiving free consulting from an experienced Indian marketing professional while in Korea.

What a full, blessed day! Following God is the **GREAT path.**

Chapter 17

He Directs Your Path, You Don't! (Day 9)

In his heart a man plans his course,
but the Lord determines his steps
PROVERBS 16:9

It was Friday, the last full day of the Lausanne Conference. I was on a bus headed to the event, seated next to a man who clearly wasn't interested in conversation. I felt disappointed because I enjoy meeting new people on these rides. The alone time allowed me to think of how in two days, on Sunday, I was traveling to another conference in South Korea. However, I was feeling unprepared for the trip to China after that, only six days away. For months I have waited to buy my flight to China, but I kept feeling God whispering for me to wait. This was unsettling, as I never travel this way, always booking travel months in advance. As I sat there in the bus seat, I sensed God speaking to me, giving specific instructions. To change my plans, skipping the second conference and buying a flight to leave in just two days—on Sunday—and spending Monday through Wednesday in Beijing, praying and fasting for the nation of China. Specifically, He wanted me in Tiananmen Square on Tuesday to pray.

This came as a shock. Essentially, God was telling me to not go to the second conference I had planned on attending and head to China earlier, with no place to stay and no clear plan other than prayer. I asked Him for confirmation, wondering if I'd heard Him correctly.

As I mulled this over, a man behind me on the bus was on the phone speaking in a language I didn't understand, but I clearly heard the words *China, church* and a third word. That was the confirmation I needed. I would skip the second Korean conference and leave for China on Sunday. I began searching for flights and hotels, then I remembered a conversation I had with a Chinese friend who mentioned there was an upcoming national holiday that week. Curious, I searched online and found that Tuesday, October 1st—just a few days away and the day God wanted me in the heart of China—marked the 75th anniversary of the founding of the People's Republic of China. It became clear that God wanted me in Beijing, in Tiananmen Square, in prayer alone with Him, at this crucial time. What added to the mystery of this was that last summer God had me travel to Israel during their 75th anniversary. I was again in a state of awe thinking of what is happening.

China: Confirmed by God

When the bus reached the conference venue, I spoke to the man who was behind me, that had been talking about China. His name was Masuru, the president of a small Christian university in Japan. He couldn't recall exactly why he mentioned China and the church, but he said he had a few Chinese students at his school. I felt led to pray for him, so we went to the cafeteria where he shared his struggles as the president of a small Christian university in a country where very few people are believers. He had to fill many roles at the school and it was draining him dry. I prayed for him, and felt God's presence strongly, guiding me to pray for his hands and feet as a symbol of his calling. When I stopped praying and was sitting across from him again, he just stared at me, thanking me, and told me that this moment was the best part of the conference for him.

Family of God = Encouragement

Later, I spent time with Jala, a friend from Uganda, a speaker whom I had been encouraging for months. She is called to bring the light of Christ into the workplace, especially in Africa, where corruption is rampant. She explained how people go to church on Sunday, then often engage in bribery and illegal activities during the week at work. Her message is about living out faith consistently, every day, not just on Sundays. We had prayed together over video calls in the past, but now I was with her face to face, what joy! She shared stories of her childhood, including how she started working at age 15, carrying water on her head for a family of twelve. Despite the hardship, her attitude and love for the families she delivered water to made an impact.

While praying together, Jala felt led to read Psalm 89 over me. Neither of us knew what it said, but as we read through the passage, she stopped me at verses 19-21:

Once you spoke in a vision, to your faithful people you said: 'I have bestowed strength on a warrior; I have exalted a young man from among the people. I have found David my servant; with my sacred oil I have anointed him. My hand will sustain him; surely my arm will strengthen him.'

Reading those words, I was overwhelmed. It reminded me of Easter Sunday 2019, when my wife anointed me with oil when we were praying at my place of work. On that day I felt God's power and calling; to lead in the workplace and to talk with government leaders. The Holy Spirit's power surged through me — stronger than anything I had ever experienced. I felt I could break tables and lift cars. It was amazing. The passage brought me back to that moment, reminding me not to fear the sudden change in plans. God was guiding me to China, and I had to follow, trusting He would guide me.

As I reflected on this, another passage from Luke 18:29-30 came to mind:

No one who has left home or wife or brothers or parents or children for the sake of the kingdom of God will fail to receive many times as much in this age and, in the age to come, eternal life.

Here I was in Korea. Praying with someone from Uganda. Far from home, family, and friends, yet surrounded by the rich blessings of God. My heart was flooded with joy and utter amazement. What God promises is true. He was providing for me.

A text then came from Heather, someone I had met a few months earlier. We had talked over a video call previously, but never actually met, and she was attending the conference. We met in the lobby and had a chance to talk and pray together. She lifted up my trip to China, encouraging me, and powerfully prayed for me. He is constantly lifting us up when He knows we need it, like I did at that moment, often in the most miraculous and unexpected ways.

It was still morning, and so far God had changed the travel plans, and done so many unplanned amazing things! All blessings, but it is overwhelming at times just following Him, as the plans kept changing minute by minute.

He determines our steps; we do not.

Chapter 18

Heart Surgery Needed

Jesus loved Martha and her sister and Lazarus
JOHN 11:5

Beth was gliding down the winter slopes of Colorado snowboarding, the crisp air and sun-soaked peaks framing what seemed like a perfect day. In her 30s and in wonderful health, with a life many would envy — thriving career, loving husband, and endless adventures — everything felt right. After a few amazing runs, she decided to take a break at the lodge, savoring a quiet moment while her husband headed out for one more descent down the mountain.

Her life was saved by that decision.

She wouldn't know it until later, but staying in the lodge had helped her sidestep death. Later that day events occurred, and now she was in a hospital bed, the doctor beside her saying, *You are lucky to be alive, your heart failed.*

A machine hummed beside her. That is what was keeping her alive. A new heart was the only thing that could save her now, but there was no guarantee one would come, and it needed to happen in days.

Beth did receive a new heart.

Over lunch, on the ten-year anniversary, we reflected on the miracle of her receiving a donor heart, a full transplant, a second life. In Beth's words, *I grew up being a believer; this changed me into being a follower.*

Her new heart is actually physically larger than her original heart, how appropriate! All of us need a new heart, the *larger* heart of Jesus, full of His radical love for people. We do not need a partially new heart; but a full heart transplant.

WARNING!
This chapter will challenge you.
Loving like Jesus is just as foreign to most of us a having a heart transplant. Yet, this is the necessary path.

HEART SURGERY NEEDED: GET READY!
Do you love others deeply like Jesus?
What kind of love did Jesus even have?

There are two key aspects:
- Loving like Jesus
- Courage: Fear of God or man?

The first is about understanding what love is, Jesus' compassionate love. The second, is if you have the courage go through with the heart surgery. The surgery will challenge us to answer the question of, who do we fear more; God and His mandate to love, or fearing what people think. Sadly, most of us fear what others think more than what God thinks. This restricts us from experiencing the best life that He promised.

What is Love?
Is it just physical intimacy? Romantic? Is that what the Bible tells us in this verse in John 11:5?
Jesus loved Martha and her sister and Lazarus.

Face it, most of us do not even know what love is. Our culture has warped our view of love. It is distorted, like looking at a mirror that is deformed, what you see — the reflection, is not reality. In many cultures, expressing caring love for others is often met with suspicion. Love is frequently misjudged, with motives questioned and misunderstood as usually assumed to be sexual in nature. Media narratives only fuel this fear, which has caused many leaders and entire churches to avoid showing deep love altogether, out of fear of judgment and being accused. This has led many in the world to look at God's Church with a sneer. Our leader Jesus gave us just *one new command*, it is not optional, we have to do this, John 13:34 says,

Heart Surgery Needed

A new command I give you: love one another.
*As I have loved you, so you **must love one another.***

We appear as hypocrites for not doing this. This Bible passage gets even more convicting, as in the next verse it says: *By this, all men will know that you are my disciples, if you love one another.* The world does not see us as followers, disciples of Jesus, as we do not love others like He did. It isn't our knowledge; it is our love, that shows we are Jesus' followers.

No wonder the world is not drawn to God. This reality should disturb us. The world around us is starving for the love that Jesus demonstrated, yet many believers fail to offer it, *making God sad.* As we fail to obey and love, we never obtain the fulfilling abundant life that Jesus promises in John 10:10, the Best Life Ever, *making us sad.* The enemy understands the power of love and does everything possible to prevent us from embracing it. Our enemy knows it will transform the world, and transform us – love is the ultimate power. A lady in Poland, a Ukrainian refugee, said to me, *you have a power,* this was after telling her and her friend about the love of Jesus for well over an hour, and praying for them. She had seen the power of God's love. Let us be wise, God's love is powerful, as stated by Reverend Dr Martin Luther King Jr saying,

I am convinced that love
is the most durable power in the world.

God wants to give you Power. It is Love.

In 1 Corinthians 12, it talks about the dozens of special gifts and callings God gives His people, including wisdom, knowledge, being an apostle, prophet, pastor, teacher, healing and miraculous powers. Wow! Then Paul the Apostle says this at the end of the chapter, 1 Corinthians 12:31, *But eagerly desire the greater gifts, and now I will show you the most excellent way.* So, what are the greater gifts we should desire? What is this most excellent way? He answers those questions in 1 Corinthians 13, where he states that even knowing all things, having power to move mountains, serving and dying for your faith are nothing compared to having love...*the greatest of these is love.* (1

93

Corinthians 13:13) You want God's power? You want a good life? Then you want lots of His love!

Our 21-year-old son offered a profound insight. He said:
> *Dad, if you show deep love for a woman, people will call you an adulterer. If you show deep love for a man, they will call you gay. So, if you follow the world's standards, you will end up loving no one, disobeying God, and having a shallow life. Dad, love like God calls you to love, not like the world.*

Loving Like Jesus
Anyone who does not love remains in death
1 JOHN 3:14

To not love is death. To live, we *must* love. Obtaining Christ's merciful heart is impossible on our own. We need a complete transformation, a new heart, just as Beth did. Her new heart was a donor's heart. Someone had to die, so Beth could live. Ponder this fact, death must occur to receive a new heart. Your heart will be exchanged for the merciful loving heart of Jesus. Just like Beth, the surgeon had to give her this heart, she could not get it by herself. God will do the surgery, and give you His heart, *you just have to ask.*

Men, I am speaking now to you. Most women naturally express love more profoundly than men, we struggle with love. We can learn so much from them. Do not think love is weak, I did, I was wrong.

Nothing is more powerful than love.

These last two years of my life, God has truly opened my eyes to the deep, powerful, courageous, earth moving, love – carefully placed into the heart of women. I am realizing I have loved so shallow, and through seeing how women love I see God, with all of His love and power. Their nurturing, compassionate, and also viciously protective nature reflects God's heart of love, and it's something we men must aspire to. The global Body of Christ has not fully embraced the powerful love that God has planted in women, but it's essential for fulfilling our mission as the Church, the full Body of Christ. So, look around at half of the human race, watch how they love, do the same. God is love. Love is power. You need this fuel to follow God.

To follow Christ, we must allow our hearts to be exchanged. It's not natural; it's rare, few have the courage (especially us men!). Love is surrendering to the needs of others. You become third. God, then others, then you. Women, especially mothers, do this all the time. Love is necessary if we are to reflect Christ in this world. Are you willing to ask God for His kind of love? If you do not, it is understandable, it is the most courageous thing a person can do.

Do You Love Courageously?

Jesus' love constantly broke cultural norms. The religious leaders hated Him for it, while the crowds adored Him. He touched the sick, embraced the outcasts, cared passionately for sinners, and talked alone with women of questionable backgrounds. Today, our society discourages us from loving others with profound compassion. Could this be why the Church hasn't had the impact Jesus intended? We hesitate as we often do not see others as Jesus does, and fear what others may think, it is a wall — preventing us from loving boldly.

For me, the journey toward Christ-like love accelerated during a sudden weeklong trip to the Chapel of Divine Mercy in Krakow, Poland, in early 2024. There, on a wooden pew bench, after an intense internal struggle, I took God's offer to give me His merciful heart in exchange for mine. He said He wanted all of my heart, to give me all of His heart. I had not asked for a heart exchange, just a little more love. I had not wanted all of His heart, yet I heard Him clearly make this offer. I struggled for over 30 minutes, as I knew I was fully releasing control. I feared I would care even more, tear up more frequently, and love more intensely – and that scared me, especially as a man. I wanted power, not more love! God's response was immediate, after I said *yes* to His offer to give me all of His merciful heart. He just gently whispered one word to me, *receive*. I had not realized it, as I was dialoguing with God, but all of the people had left the chapel, and others had taken their place. As I heard the word, *receive*, immediately I heard singing. Beautiful singing, all women's voices, from all around me. *What was going on?!?!* I slowly opened my eyes and brought up my gaze. In front I saw, black, black, black, I was surrounded by over 50 nuns singing in Polish. It was beautiful, I felt like I was in heaven with angels singing around me. For almost an hour I sat there, palms up and eyes closed, silently receiving this most beautiful gift. Since then, I've realized that loving others with Christ's heart means being open, vulnerable, and extremely empathetic. Being available to love those He brings to me, I cannot choose who, I just follow and love. I was transformed and my heart was exchanged. Having the merciful heart of Christ is both a gift and a challenge.

What is a Merciful Heart?

Loving with Christ's new heart comes at a cost. The day after this spiritual surgery on my heart, I met Daniel at breakfast there in Poland. He is a Catholic priest originally from Nigeria, but now serving as a Chaplain for the US Army. I told him how God is giving me all of His merciful heart, and I asked him what mercy means to him as a Priest. His eyes grew large, and with excitement he said,

> *Wow! If God is choosing to give you all of his merciful heart that is such a gift, an honor, yet it will be painful. Pope Francis said another word for God is Mercy. You are blessed. This is not an easy road though; you need to understand fully what this means. Mercy is all of love, plus the deep compassionate weeping care for others and feeling their pain intimately. As Jesus did when he saw that Lazarus had died, the pain of others will move you. It is an open heart. Full of kindness, tenderness, gentleness, generosity, and weeping with others as they hurt. You will be made extremely vulnerable. You will care so much for others it will consume your emotions. You will feel their pain as if it were your own. You will weep with them. God will need to expose you to the most painful wickedness in this world and what men have done to each other, so you will be in touch with their pain. You will weep. You will feel what they feel so you can walk with them, like Jesus did. It requires strength, which God will have to fill you with, as without it, you would be crushed. You*

*will have the merciful heart of Jesus and with that will be able
to bless and heal those hurting.*

Courage to love? Fear of Man or God?

People will criticize you, call you unorthodox, odd, weird,
and risky. You will likely be betrayed by someone you love,
which I have learned is the most horrible pain. Yet remember,
Jesus was also criticized for loving all people. Friends from
Germany and Palestine summarized this well telling me:

> *You can either fear what man says or what God commands,
> it is that simple. Even though they are religious leaders, they
> obviously are more concerned about what others think,
> instead of obeying what God in the Bible says about loving.
> Do not be like them, we need more people like you.*

This sounded exactly like what happened to Jesus in
Matthew 9. The experts in the law and scriptures, were furious
that Jesus was with and loving those the religious leaders
avoided, who were the friends of Matthew, who was to become
Matthew the Apostle. Jesus turned to these religious people and
commanded, *Go and learn what this means: I desire mercy (Matthew
9:13).* Merciful love is the true measure of our faith — not
knowledge, great speaking, or righteous acts. Unless our efforts
result in more deep love for people, it is just wasted effort. From
my vantage point we have more of a lack of love, than a lack of
knowledge or truth. Knowledge is needed of course, being the
fertile soil, but the goal is a plant bearing the fruit of love, not
just fertile soil. May we apply the words of Jesus to ourself, *Go
and learn what this means: I desire mercy.* Paul tells us in 1
Corinthians 13 *the greatest of these is love,* not knowledge,
amazing miracles or even a life with little sin. Love of others is
the fruit we desire from our lives.

Ultimately, even we who are the children of God will be
judged, giving an account of our life directly to God Himself.
(Romans 14:12, but read all of Romans 14) Imagine the day you will
stand alone before God's judgment seat to be judged
individually for your actions on earth. Pause and think about it.
This could be very intimidating, God judging me alone! I want
God to smile. What is the standard God will use to judge me?

Us? Knowing the standard is critical, it is the key to passing the test. Fortunately, God tells us, it is not a mystery. **God's standard is great love for others.** Galatians 5:14 tells us: *The entire law is summed up in a single command: "Love your neighbor as yourself."*

I've struggled to show this kind of love, I am lazy at times and don't like it when others disapprove. When I stand before God, I would be shocked if He looks at me with a frown telling me I was loving too much! Instead, likely most of us will be saddened when God asks us how we deeply loved those around us, our neighbors, as we in shame say we did not. Most of us spend more effort trying to avoid sin, which is good, but it not more important than obeying God's highest command — loving others.

I would rather risk loving too much,
than loving too little.

A Prayer for Courageous Love

This prayer has transformed my heart, pray it with me:
> *Lord Jesus, I know you want me to love all people, with mercy as you did. I need Your heart, please replace my heart with Yours. I am scared of what others may think of me as I give you control and follow, loving others. I desire to love all those you bring to me, blessing and lifting them up. I want all of your merciful, loving heart. Amen.*

God will give you a new heart and the courage to love as Jesus loved. It will take time, but step by step, you will begin to see others with the compassionate, merciful heart of Christ. You will be compelled by the love of God in you to move toward them in love, as 2 Corinthians 5:14 tells us:
> *For Christ's love compels us…*

Remember, you don't get to choose whom to love. God does. **Our role is to simply pour out lots of love!**

Now I will show you the most excellent way…
Follow the way of love.
1 CORINTHIANS 12:31, 14:1

Chapter 19

What is Your Calling?
(Day 9-continued)

Compelled by the Spirit, I am going to Jerusalem,
not knowing what will happen to me there.
ACTS 20:22

What is your purpose? What is God choosing you to do?
What is your calling?

This is a critical question to ask, know, and lean into. Without it, we have no purpose, no hope... no lasting joy. There is no way you can have the best life, if you do not know what you were created for. You have to know your calling.

It was Friday morning, at the conference, the theme of the day was *Servanthood to the Holy Spirit*. It felt particularly relevant since the Holy Spirit had just redirected my travel plans to leave to China in two days! The speaker referenced Acts 20:22, *compelled by the Spirit, I'm going to Jerusalem, not knowing what will happen to me there.* It resonated as I prepared to go to China on the 75th anniversary of the founding of the nation, with no idea what awaited me, only that God had called me. Prior to traveling to Asia, many good friends had questioned why I was even going to China, as they felt it was unsafe. My only response had been, *I felt God calling me to.* In processing this verse in Acts, I felt as Paul did, I didn't have a choice; I was compelled to go.

The speaker then asked, *How and who is God calling you to serve?* That was clear to me, my calling has been unfolding these last few years. God gives all of us a unique calling.

For me it is:

- **Pray and have Deep Merciful Love like Jesus** - I pray. Knowing God, and partnering with Him is the critical foundation. I feel overflowing compassion for people and nations, compelling me to pray.
- **Bless Women** – to see, hear, understand, lift up, love and support as daughters of the King.
- **Workplace** – open doors for people in the workplace to *Reflect God's Love @Work*. Changing workplaces, companies, and transforming nations with God's love.
- **Government** – I feel He is opening a role in the Government to reflect His love and light there, and through that I will be sent to the nations.

This is my calling, as of right now. It likely is not yours. The Bible in 1 Corinthians 12 clearly tells us God designed us each with different gifts and abilities, to make His Body, His Church whole.

> *There are different kinds of gifts but the same Spirit.*
> *There are different kinds of service, but the same Lord.*
> *There are different kinds of working, but the same God…*
> *for the common good…*
> *he gives them to each one, just as he determines.*
> 1 CORINTHIANS 12:4-6,7,11

Our callings and gifting will be different; that is part of the plan. God is the one that gives the callings – *we do not get to pick.*

God will likely give you a calling that is uncomfortable, that you didn't choose. I heard this profoundly in Poland, when at a conference a man that leads a global ministry was discussing Acts 1:8 with me in the hall, and how it was challenging him.

> *…You will be my witnesses in Jerusalem, and in all Judea*
> *and **Samaria**, and to the ends of the Earth.*

The man talked about why *Samaria* was specifically called out, stating how it is because that is the last place any good Jew would want to go. Samaritans were the outcasts, the ones you culturally do not associate or are seen with, the ones that made you feel uncomfortable, and the ones you grew up hearing bad things about. It is interesting though, as Jesus went to Samaria and spoke alone to a Samaritan woman, and she was honored to be the first one to hear that He is the Messiah, the anointed chosen one of God! God knows your heart, like He knows mine. He will likely call you to areas that feel uncomfortable, to your Samaria, and to those you prefer not to go to. God did for me, so get ready!

Looking at the list of my callings, I feel overwhelmed, all of them feel too big. Some of my calling may seem unusual to you, which is likely one of the reasons God wanted me to write this book. Let me be clear, I did not choose these callings or even initially desire them. If it was my choice, I would have selected other ones. However, now I feel very blessed to be called to these areas. I see God's love and power at work. I partner with Him, doing what He designed and created me to do, dependent on Him. For years I have heard critiques on four of these callings, such as; *deep merciful love*: it is usually not appropriate as it could lead to issues and it is too much effort; *blessing women*: a man should never do this, as only a woman can do that safely; *workplace:* is for work and a church is for things of God; *government:* a follower of Christ should never be involved in the sewage of government. I had no critiques on *prayer*, until the day when writing this chapter (what timing!) the critique was from a friend saying, *A lot of prayer could be a distraction from what God wants you to really be doing.* So, critiques on all of them, and interestingly all the people critiquing are Christians, even the critique on prayer. No Muslim, Hindu, Sikh, Atheist, or other person, only a few Christians questioned the value of these areas.

Note – God has called me to walk in these areas with freedom, power and protection. These areas may not be for you! It could be a wreck if you went into these areas, or any area where God has not called you, hurting others and yourself. You need to follow God to where He wants you to go, but being "safe" and doing nothing is not an option.

Judging another's Calling – Be Careful!

We each have unique callings, yet we are all part of the same body, as 1 Corinthians 12:12 tells us:

The body is a unit, though it is made up of many parts;
and though all its parts are many, they form one body.

Maybe I am the hand and you are the arm. It is foolish for me to look down on you as you are *just an arm*. I cannot fulfill my purpose as a hand, if you are not fulfilling yours as the arm. You need me. I need you. We truly all need each other. The challenge though, is it is natural to think of ourselves as having the *right or best* calling, as that is what we understand. This is why we must be careful not to judge, God knows what He is doing!

Jesus warned against this, and the Apostle Paul spells it out bluntly. We must be careful to judge another; *who are you to judge someone else's servant? (Romans 14:4).* We can and should though look at the fruit of the action (*Is the fruit love, for the other person?*). Yet we must be careful judging the heart or the method. The religious leaders in Jesus' day did that, and He was harsh with them. God will judge our heart, our motives, our methods. We can only judge by what we see through the lens of our limited perspective, culture and tradition. Each of us is called to our unique calling, and others are called to theirs. Often, we will not understand their value, as we only understand and see the value of our own calling. Paul says this in his own words in 1 Corinthians 4:2-5, where the word *trust* and *calling* are similar.

Now it is required that those who have been given a trust must prove faithful. I care very little if I am judged by you or by any human court; indeed, I do not even judge myself. My conscience is clear, but that does not make me innocent. It is the Lord who judges me. Therefore, judge nothing before the appointed time; wait until the Lord comes. He will bring to light what is hidden in darkness and will expose the motives of the heart. At that time each will receive their praise from God.

Are you Wicked and Worthless?

These words sting. They hurt even to write, but this is Jesus' perspective, His words, and we must listen. These words are addressed to those that avoid risk, and do not fulfill their calling.

What is Your Calling?

Jesus speaks harshly in Matthew 25:14-30, where He tells a story about three servants that are each given money to invest. As anyone who invests knows, to get higher returns it requires higher risk. The master was expecting high returns! One servant was fearful, burying the money safely in the dirt. He didn't want to risk losing the money. The man's master in the story, representing God, strongly reprimands this fearful risk adverse person that did not take action, calling him a *wicked lazy servant*:

...throw the worthless servant outside, into the darkness, where there will be weeping and gnashing of teeth.

We must take action to fulfill our calling.
This will always include risk.

If there is no risk, you are burying both your talents and your calling. Then expect the fate of the wicked worthless servant.

This should terrify most of us! Most of us are *comfortable cowards*. That fully includes me at times. Is there very little that could ever go wrong, because you are fearful of taking risks? You should be more fearful of what may happen if you do not fulfill your calling... *darkness, weeping, gnashing of teeth*. Yes, you may make a mistake as you seek to fulfill your calling, sin even. Maybe the two other servants failed a few times as they successfully fulfilled their calling to invest the money. In this story, Jesus only criticized the one that had fear and took no action. In Christian circles we have removed the word *fearful* and replaced it with nicer terms, calling fear and lack of action being *prudent, cautious, wise* or *practical*. You do not want to be the wicked worthless servant who failed to take action. God wants us to fulfill His call, which gives merciful love like Jesus, this will always take courage.

*Courage is action in spite of fear.
Be courageous! Invest, take the risk, fulfill your calling!*

How do I know my Calling?

You have one. Do you know it? It will give you purpose, and direction. Fulfilling it is the only way you will hear God tell you, *Well done!* Years ago, I heard a sermon on how you can easily understand God's call for your life. It is understanding what breaks your heart. What moves you? Hurts so intensely? The Pastor had shared how he dislikes abortion, but it doesn't break his heart. Yet, when he sees a homeless person addicted to drugs on the street, his hear weeps and breaks. That is his calling, to lean in and serve in this area. What is yours?

What breaks your heart?

Take some time here. Do not keep reading until you have thought on this and processed what areas truly break your heart. Others may not understand, that is fine, God gives us each a unique calling and He desires us to then take action.

Need to get Dirty

To fulfill your call, the Lausanne conference speaker reminded us we have to enter the tough, dirty world of those we are called to serve, just as Jesus entered the world in Bethlehem, born as a baby in a dirty stable used for animals. It will be ugly and challenging, and with that there is risk and a chance of failure. Sitting on the safe couch is not an option for a follower of Jesus. A question you may ask is, *what if in the process of serving people, I make a mistake, disobeying God sinning and hurting someone?* Fair question. Do we think that God would rather we isolate ourselves from the sin and muck of the world, to avoid any mistake? Was that what Jesus and His followers did? No, He and his followers entered this dirty world to help and to love. I firmly believe the greater mistake, the greater sin that God will critically judge, is our inaction. Failing periodically as we actively try to fulfill our calling to love and bless, is better than doing nothing and being safe. I would much rather follow Him 100 times; succeeding 95 times, and failing miserably five times, instead of being safe and not serving once out of fear of the 5% chance of failure. I am fearful of what God will say to me if I do not follow my calling. I would rather fail trying, than not to try at all. We have to enter their world, and lay down our life for them, it is dirty and you will be tempted. You may fail. Only one man, King David, was described by God *as a man after My own heart (Acts 13:22)*, yet David was tempted and failed horribly a few times in his life. David though was a person of action, he repented, followed God, and God was very pleased. The Lausanne speaker continued saying, you have a choice, either to fear God or fear man. Do you want to influence by following God? Or, is your focus to please and impress man? Ultimately, the speaker wrapped it up by asking the question.

Who are you trying to please?

Emptied to be Filled

I have often struggled with the fear of man, wondering what people think of me when I follow God's leading, especially when He calls me to unexpected places and to love compassionately all He brings to me. Others frequently do not understand. I love very intentionally as Jesus did, and I am finding out this is quite unusual! I really do care so much about people, I see and feel their pain, and also glimpse the glorious masterpiece that God desires them to be.

It was not over though, the speaker continued to talk about how Paul writes in Philippians 2:3-8. How Jesus humbled himself, and He emptied himself. The speaker said,

...you will know you are empty
when you are consumed by the love for others,
because that is the love of Jesus fully filling you

Yes, that is how I feel! I look at people and act differently now, consumed with love. These are often people I don't even really know, yet I care so greatly for them. The recipients of this love always feel seen, blessed, and loved by God. I have surrendered myself to focus on pleasing God first. With this choice, it makes the following much easier. There is no *Plan B*. Like Spanish Cortez burning his ships upon reaching the New World, making the only path forward his calling into Mexico.

I did not choose my calling, God did.
Even if in fear, even with risk, **I WILL fulfill my calling.**

Chapter 20

Women of Valor
(Day 9-even more)

I sent Moses to lead you, also Aaron and Miriam.
MICAH 6:4

Women of Valor was the name of an afternoon small group session. Of the 5,000 people at the conference, there were 30 women present, along with two men, one being me. Obviously, not the most popular topic at the conference. The women expressed gratitude that a couple of men had joined, wishing more had attended. During the session, I once again witnessed the pain many women experience — often feeling marginalized or hurt by society or the church. The focus on physical beauty and the feeling of walls blocking them from leadership roles were recurring themes. Key takeaways were:

1) A woman's heart needs healing

Many women are deeply wounded. I firmly believe that men play an important role in the healing process. While I've seen the profound impact of women praying for each other, when a man lovingly prays over a woman, it often seems as though the gates of heaven open, pouring healing and blessing into her heart. There's something powerful about a woman receiving God's love poured through a man, a fatherly figure, as it reminds her of the love of our heavenly Father. It can heal many of the wounds originally inflicted by a man. God's rich love is needed to heal a wounded heart.

2) Women need to see their own value

This was a surprising revelation for me as a man. I've always viewed women as having incredible worth. Many women don't see themselves this way, often because culture and even Christian structures have not recognized their worth and contribution, making them feel like second-class citizens.

3) Commissioning is needed to fulfill their purpose

Women need to realize they have a mandate from God to achieve something significant. Having someone in authority acknowledge this and call them forward to fulfill it is important. When a man is the one to do this, it can be even more powerful.

4) The world will change

I saw the immense power of love in women's hearts during a small women's conference in Poland in early 2024, where I was volunteering. The depth of love, compassion, and care on display was awe-inspiring. This conference was more profound and powerful than any of the dozens of conferences I had been to, all because it was women only. It struck me that this love I saw in that room was one of the best reflections of God, and it is naturally embedded in the heart of a woman. That is POWER sealed up in the loving hearts of women, that the world just doesn't see or understand. When women are empowered and unleashed, working closely with men, this love has the power to transform every sphere they enter. It's a force the church and world need to recognize and fuel. The greatest power in the world is love, and women have been gifted with it naturally.

A Bridge to Connect

My mind was overwhelmed from the session, and I was needing time to process all of this. I was walking to the next event with my mind spinning, and met a group of people walking the same direction, one was a lady named Steph. We had just introduced ourselves when she suddenly stopped in the hall and said, *I really need to pray for you, right now.* She prayed, *I see you as a bridge with a very heavy weight on top of you. But God is with you, strengthening you. Many will walk over you as you connect them, building relationships of peace. You will connect and support many.* Wow, I didn't expect that! A few months earlier, during a prayer meeting at my church, a lady had seen a heavy load on me—an immense, human-crushing burden. A weight so heavy she could not comprehend it. The weight was the calling that God had called me to. However, she also saw that God would sustain me and strengthen me so that the load would feel like a feather as God would carry the load and I was to walk forward with great joy, rejoicing. Now my mind truly could not process all of this, and I needed a place to sit, and it wasn't even lunchtime yet!

God Providing a Family

I sat in the hallway and a man stopped by, and we struck up a conversation, Kaarti, originally from India. He's been living in the U.S. for over 30 years and is an engineering professor in Washington state. He's in his late 40s, and had been married just a few years. He and his wife have no children. He shared how he had been offered a job as the president of a university and was praying about whether to accept. We prayed together, and I felt led to share Mark 10:29-30 with him: *I tell you the truth, no one who has left home or family for me and the gospel will fail to receive a hundred times as much.*

I felt God was telling him not to take the position. Instead, God was going to bless him through his students, who would become like his children. I saw him as a lion—gentle, yet viciously protective of these students. He would have wonderful relationships with them, watching them marry and have children, loving them as his own. When I opened my eyes, my professor friend was in tears. He told me this is exactly how he feels about his students. He also shared that the verse I had quoted was the same one read over him when he was baptized, decades prior. The pastor had said it would be true in his life, but Kaarti had never fully understood how—until now. It was a divine moment, and I praised God for allowing me to be part of it. God though wanted to add to this blessing. As we sat quietly there in the hall, reflecting on how God had just moved. My friend Mandisa appeared with a big smile and a beautifully wrapped gift for my wife; it was vanilla from Madagascar, where she is from. I was so touched. God's blessings just kept coming.

Secure Communications Needed

Running late now, I rushed to the meeting place where I was meeting a man named Tani, a businessman from the small country of Brunei. Brunei is a very small Asian oil-rich nation controlled by a Muslim family. How I had met him a few days prior was absolutely miraculous, and today I would get to speak to him more. A few days ago, when I was helping to facilitate the meeting for the 1,500 people in the workplace track, the Korean volunteer coordinator approached me. Using her phone to translate, she said there was a man out in the hall who wanted to know some specific information about a bus. We had no bus. I was ready to ignore him as I was busy, but God said to go with her to speak to that man. The man was Tani, the man I would now be meeting with. I was unsure why God was wanting me to meet him, I would soon learn. We sat down and he introduced me to two others, Miguel and Daisy. Miguel, I learned is the founder of a global set of groups that works privately with Christian leaders in senior government and business roles. They work to help their nations to grow, by successfully leveraging Christ's principles. We had a wonderful discussion, and I realized the absolute need for a global secure platform, which is what the Courageous Third tool would offer to people like Miguel and others.

Family can be challenging – God provides

At that meeting, I also met Daisy, who is from the US. I felt that we should talk more, so Daisy and I quickly rushed to the dining hall right as they were closing. We talked about many things, but the most amazing thing was that she felt led to pray for me, suddenly stating, *I see you at the forefront of politics.* We had just met, she had no idea that for the few months prior to this, God has been nudging me and opening amazing doors in the government area. She also gave me helpful advice on how to handle some challenging family relational issues with my extended family, as she had walked a similar path. We talked about the cost of following God, and she shared how even those close to us can persuade us to not follow the path that God wants for our lives.

Co-Conquerors

As the day wrapped up, I reflected on how I was the recipient of the wisdom and blessing from many women throughout the day. Men and women have to work closely together; we are co-conquerors of the earth, designed to have different complementary roles. May we not shy away from the strategy God originally planned. The world needs to see the love of God.

> *God created mankind in his own image, in the image of God*
> *he created them; male and female he created them.*
> *God blessed them and said to them,*
> *"Be fruitful and increase in number; fill the earth*
> ***and subdue it. Rule over***
> *the fish and the birds in the sky and*
> *over every living thing...*
> *GENESIS 1:27-28*

Chapter 21

Message from God
(Day 10)

*Joshua was near Jericho, he looked up and saw a man
standing in front of him with a drawn sword...
Joshua fell face down in reverence and asked him,
"What message does my Lord have for his servant?"*
JOSHUA 5:13-14

God will frequently give us a message. Are you ready to receive it? It will likely not be with an angel holding a drawn sword, but He will prepare you if you are ready to listen.

Some do not believe God still speaks to us personally; well, then they should expect to hear nothing. The Bible is filled with constant God and human communication from cover to cover. We should expect God to communicate to us now, as God does not change, *I the Lord do not change (Malachi 3:6)*. Get ready though when He does speak, as you will see.

Leaving 25 Year Career
Today was the last day of the Lausanne conference. What timing, as I will never forget what happened exactly two years prior. On that day, I was told by my management at Intel that my role, along with thousands of others, was being eliminated. They offered me a retirement and separation package, and without hesitation, I accepted. Before the meeting ended, I asked my managers if I could pray for them. I had been a manager and had to deliver this same news to my employees, it is always difficult for a manager. Neither of them follow Jesus, so they were stunned by my request, and just stared at me speechless.

111

As someone who had just lost his job, I realized they could not tell me no, so I went ahead and prayed for God's blessing on them. My wife stood beside me, in shock, as we faced the close of this 25-year chapter at Intel. Yet, I was filled with confidence. It stemmed from the fact that God had miraculously prepared me for this moment four weeks earlier, giving me a message, just like the angel had given Joshua a message. God had foretold that something like this would occur, so I was emotionally ready.

God can Prepare us for Change

Four weeks prior to my job being eliminated, I was in a product management video call meeting about my product. While I wasn't asked a single question, I left feeling completely out of place. I had a successful career as a product manager, with increasing responsibility over time, and now for products generating $2 billion in lifetime revenue. I was in a great position — but it was not my calling and everything inside of me knew it. My heart was heavy, and I knew this role was slowly choking me.

Immediately after that meeting, I fell to my knees, pressing my face into the carpet, and prayed. I told God I wouldn't get up until He did something, because my heart felt like it was dying. I even noted the exact time in my journal — 11:08 AM — thinking I would be there all day. God, with His perfect sense of humor, answered almost instantly. I had barely been on the floor for 20 seconds when I heard His voice: *Prayer answered. Door opened. Get up. Stop praying.* I was stunned. I had just poured my heart out to God, asking Him to change things, and in a matter of seconds, He responded. That is normally not what happens.

I sat on the couch, opened my journal, and filled nearly two pages with what God was telling me. The message came in three parts. The first reaffirmed His caring love for me: *I heard you. I love you. I will take care of you. Follow me. Rejoice, for great is your reward.* His words were full of comfort and reassurance.

The second part was more direct: He told me I would be leaving Intel. *You will succeed and win. The path is straight. The road is smooth. Now is the time to go, to fly. I am with you. Stand firm. Be a man of courage. Go forward.* I was in awe—God was launching me into a new chapter. The third part, which I will not go into detail about, was about war, death, conflict, and devastation, but also victory and safety. Especially this third part was difficult to hear, but I knew it was somehow part of the journey He had me on.

So, when my job was eliminated exactly two years ago, I had peace. God had promised this moment, and He had given me hope and joy for what was to come. Now, as I sit in Korea at an incredible conference where God is using me to bless people from all over the world, I can see that His ways truly are mysterious, but they are always the best path. Over the past two years, others have asked countless times, *What are you doing? What's your plan?* I often felt embarrassed by my response, as I am even a certified Project Manager, I know how to plan! My response could only be: *I'm following God, and I know I'm exactly where I'm supposed to be, even though nothing has happened as I had planned.* A few people understand, but most simply smile politely, likely thinking I was a bit odd and felt sorry for me.

Others will not Understand

One wise friend, Sam, who leads an Intel Christian group in California, gave me some advice I'll never forget. I had been venting to him about how frustrating it was that others didn't understand what God was calling me to do. Sam's words were simple and profound:

> *You heard the voice of God. They didn't. You can't expect them to fully understand or share your excitement.*

Those words have stayed with me, a reminder that following God's call can be a lonely path, but also an intimate path as you partner and walk alone with Him. Others may not understand the message, but God will make sure you do.

Listen—He may be sending you a message.

Chapter 22

Loving Deeply
(Day 10-continued)

And what does the Lord require of you?
To act justly, to love mercy and
to walk humbly with your God.
MICAH 6:8

On the final bus ride to the conference, I found myself reflecting on how God had unexpectedly woken me up at 5 AM to speak with our two boys via a video call, and then with my wife. When technology works, it truly feels miraculous. In almost 30 years of marriage, that may have been the most meaningful fun-loving hour-long conversation I've ever had with my sweet wife over the phone. I felt overwhelmed with love and blessing, almost dancing around the hotel room, having spoken to my family before leaving for this adventure to China. Praise God that the day prior my new friend Daisy had given me advice on some things to talk to our boys about, how we need other followers of Jesus in our life! I was relieved to have talked to them as I wasn't sure what might happen during my journey, and I wanted to have a heartfelt conversation before leaving. I had. I was satisfied and joy-filled.

Now, on the bus, heading to the last day of the conference I was sitting next to Natalia, a woman from a former Soviet republic in Asia. She shared her story of being imprisoned by the KGB for three days because of her Christian faith. Years prior, God had broken her heart with compassion for the people in need in her area, mostly women, and she was determined to do something about this. Her husband, steadfastly supported

114

her call, encouraging her to be courageous in her faith and leadership. Without him, she told me, she would have stopped years ago, she is reliant on his support. Natalia explained how in her culture, women are expected to follow, not lead. Yet she knew God had designed her to be a leader, so she leads, despite constant cultural and religious pressure not to. She works at an incredible organization, and on the side, helps people through trauma counseling. For 26 years, she's been dedicated to helping the weak, answering God's call to serve people all over the world. She has courage!

Loving is One on One

Today, I needed to figure out where to leave one of my bags, as I felt led to travel light in China. I had peace, knowing that if God had called me to China, He could provide a place for me to leave my larger suitcase. At the conference hall I approached the table where the Korean volunteers were stationed. A man assisted me, while a young woman who spoke broken English, watched. After I finished speaking with the man, I felt prompted by God to speak to the woman, Jee-Hee. I asked how she was doing and if I could pray for her, she looked surprised and began to tear up, and asked if we could step aside to talk. She was about the same age as our two sons. She shared that she had just broken up with her boyfriend the day before as felt they were not pursuing God enough. I was blessed to pray for her relationship with God and for healing from her breakup. Through tears, she asked me, like so many others have,

Who are you? Are you a pastor?

I smiled and said,

No, not exactly – just a brother in Christ
who loves to minister and pray for people.

I felt incredibly blessed by the opportunity to pray with her. Go God! We are all His pastors and ministers.

Later, during this last main session, there was a lot of discussion about love and caring for others, about how we should pray and support each other. In the middle of the session, I received a text message from a friend in another country, struggling with depression and even contemplating suicide, feeling as though God had abandoned them. I was faced with a choice: stay in the last session and respond later, or act now? What would Jesus do? God sent His Son to comfort and heal those in need, so I knew I had to act immediately. I left the session, walked out in front of thousands, and made the call. It was a long conversation filled with tears, but by the end, my friend felt that God still cared — because He had sent me to deliver His caring compassion on that call. We are called to be His hands and His voice. What if I had hesitated? Love requires action. If there is no action, can it really be called love?

Feeling God loves you is priceless. Hearing those words that *God loves you* coming from another person of flesh and bone is so necessary. Jesus came as a human, a man, so we could relate to Him. It is the same way when we interact with the people around us, they need a person to talk to, to look at, to compassionately care for them. That afternoon my heart was beyond blessed and I could feel the love of God flowing through me to my friend in need, and in the process I in turn also felt incredibly seen and cared for by God. Walking back into the conference though, my heart was in pain. I had heard much talk about caring and love over the days of the conference. Yet it was clear, few people knew how to deliver it, or desired to deliver this sort of deep care in a one-on-one fashion. I had heard so many times; *the highlight of the conference was our talk and how you prayed for me.* I know I am called to do this. Yet, I struggle to think that not everyone is also called to do this at least a little. Ultimately though, that is between them and God. I know what I have been called to do. The Bible passage from John 12 came to mind — where Mary shows extravagant love for Jesus, breaking cultural norms by pouring expensive perfume on His hair and feet and wiping His feet with her hair. Many were shocked and outraged, but Jesus said, *leave her alone.* Loving deeply often defies human logic and cultural expectations. I pray that we all have the courage to love profoundly like Mary.

Lausanne Covenant

At the Lausanne Conference, we signed a covenant to fulfill the Great Commission, promote unity, and support the younger generation. It was a beautiful moment, with people from Latvia, Uganda, and India at my table, signing my document with me. At that moment, with over 5,000 believers from 180 nations worshiping God together, I felt an overwhelming sense of blessing and unity in Christ.

Humbled by Pain to Bless

On the bus back to the hotel, I sat next to a pastor from Kenya. As we talked, his face grew sadder and sadder as he shared his struggles. Married with children, he and his wife had desired another child. In the last few years, they had suffered five miscarriages, and three of their four parents had passed away unexpectedly. As a pastor in a church where every prayer is expected to be answered, this left him doubting God and questioning himself as a pastor. Yet, through this pain, his heart had been humbled, as God had not answered his prayers. This gave him profound empathy and compassion for others. He could not see that, but I sure could! His broken heart flowed with the compassionate love of Jesus. We held hands, and I prayed with him, thanking God for the gift of empathy that would enable him to minister to others in profound ways. He told me he had never shared this with anyone before, which broke my heart. How often do we fail to create spaces where people feel safe to share their pain?

A Big Sister! Joy!

After the pastor left the bus, I got another sister! Yes - more sisters are always welcome! A woman from Kenya wearing bright traditional clothing and with a huge smile filled the empty seat next to me, and we struck up a conversation. By the time we got to the hotel, we were laughing and calling each other brother and sister. We shared such joy during the ride. As we reached the hotel, I felt overflowing with gratitude. So many moments of fellowship and community that occurred nonstop during my time at the 4th Lausanne Conference in South Korea.

When you follow Jesus, loving others like Jesus, **you receive amazing friendship and love from Jesus, through His Body!**

Chapter 23

Hearing His Voice

...the sheep listen to his voice. He calls his own sheep by
name and leads them out... he goes on ahead of them,
and his sheep follow him because they know his voice.
JOHN 10:3-4

Hearing God's voice is absolutely critical. It is the only way to follow well. Just like sheep, if sheep do not hear and obey, the shepherd uses a staff to hit them and poke them — you do not want that! When God opens a door, we should be ready to walk through it, but not every time. As our Shepherd, He calls us to listen carefully to His voice. Even when a door seems wide open, it's crucial to discern God's specific direction before stepping forward. This requires an intimate relationship with Him to understand His will. Should we go through every open door? No, we are called to follow, so it depends on what God tells us to do. Hearing His voice is key, and to do that you have to deeply know Him.

Should we Always Run Through an Open Door?
A few years ago, while working at Intel, I led a project to create a platform that allowed employees to form and join religious and faith-based groups at work. This initiative would foster authenticity in employees' faith while benefiting the company in three key areas: recruitment, retention, and overall returns — what I call the *Three R's of Benefit*. I had received support from 15 vice-presidents, including a key staff member reporting directly to the CEO, and there was talk of funding. Everything pointed to a wide-open door, one that seemed like it

was from God. In excitement, I was talking to God during my morning prayer time, I distinctly heard God say,
Wait. Now is not the time.
The pieces and the people are not ready yet.

It was a confusing moment. I did not want to hear that! All the signs suggested that God had opened this door — there was enthusiasm, potential funding, and the potential for great Godly global impact. It felt like God was asking me to sit down on the racetrack stopping, just short of reaching the finish line. I felt disappointed, extremely frustrated, and even embarrassed – as I, along with so many others, were looking forward to it. Yet, I obeyed. Looking back now, I understand why. The timing wasn't right, and though it seemed like perfect timing to me, God knew the pieces weren't fully in place. The lesson? Just because a door is open doesn't mean God wants you to walk through it. We must be sure that it is God who is leading you to step through. We have to hear His voice.

When God says, *GO!*

The story of this 40-day journey to Asia and Washington D.C. began in the month of May, with Raymond, who opened the door for me to embark on this adventure. I felt God telling me to go, and I asked for confirmation. That same day I unexpectedly received an invitation forwarded from a friend for a second conference in South Korea. I heard God say to go to Asia.

A month later, in June, while vacationing in Mexico with my family, I felt God prompting me to attend a conference in Dallas in the USA immediately after our vacation. My wife thought it was crazy — and she wasn't wrong. The day after we arrived home, I was on a flight to the conference, with lodging and flights I booked when on vacation. Following God often involves stepping into what seems unusual.

At the Dallas Faith at Work Conference, I met Joseph, the Lausanne Movement's workplace leader. He introduced me to a small volunteer team that would be supporting over 40 speakers for the workplace track, which would have over 1,500 attendees. Suddenly, Joseph asked me in front of a few of them if I had any project management experience from my time at Intel. I told him I did and mentioned that I was even certified as a project manager. To my surprise, he asked me to lead the volunteer team, help manage the speakers from 30 countries, and facilitate the publication of their talks in a book. Though it seemed overwhelming, I felt a clear prompting from God to say *yes*, so I did.

Working with this amazing team of volunteers was a true blessing, dear brothers and a sister. Many times, we prayed together, and I had the privilege of praying with many of the speakers as well in our twice-weekly prayer calls or in 1:1 meetings. Many of the speakers became cherished brothers and sisters in Christ. When we finally met face-to-face at the South Korea conference, it felt like a glorious family reunion.

Blessings happen when we just follow.

Chapter 24

Angel and a Prisoner (Day 11)

He has sent me to bind up the brokenhearted,
to proclaim freedom for the captives
ISAIAH 61:1

It was my last day in Korea before heading to China. I wanted to take a long walk before going to the airport, so I put on some shorts, a white long-sleeved hooded shirt to protect me from the sun, and a blue sweatshirt over it. Just as I stepped out of my hotel, I remembered there might be free breakfast available. I felt a nudge from God to go have breakfast, even though I had planned to fast that morning, skipping the meal. I couldn't shake the feeling, so I went to try to have breakfast.

When I arrived at the breakfast area, I was two minutes late. The woman there frowned and said I had missed breakfast, but then, surprisingly, she let me sit anyway. I was grateful, realizing that small miracles were already unfolding—and it wouldn't be the last one that day. As I picked up my food, I scanned the room for a place to sit. Two ladies nearby were chatting and laughing, looking like they were having a great time. I almost joined them, but then I noticed a man sitting alone, staring down at his empty plate, looking sad. That's when I felt God nudging me again, this time to sit with him.

Called to China: Needing an Angelic Sign

The man's name was Esmael, from a country in Africa. He told me how a year ago, he felt God calling him to get his PhD in finance—in China, of all places. He had been there for eight

121

months, separated from his wife and three young children, and the loneliness was crushing him. Esmael shared how he had spent the last few days in tears, questioning if he had made a mistake, feeling as if God had abandoned him. Despite all this, Esmael told me how, during his time in China, he had been blessed to see 44 people come to know the love of Jesus due to his presence there. Also, he told me how his heart was moved with love to pray for China, fasting and praying frequently for the nation. I mentioned to him that this same day I would travel to China, which amazed us both. Esmael had been praying for China for months, and I was also being sent there to pray! I was amazed again at God's orchestration of details.

As he spoke, I began to feel warm, so I took off my blue sweatshirt, revealing the bright shiny white long-sleeve hooded nylon shirt beneath. Esmael's eyes grew wide, and he started crying. He then told me that he had been praying for an angel to appear and encourage him. While I'm certainly no angel, I realized that God had placed me there to be an answer to his prayer, on the exact day I would be flying to China. Over breakfast, I took his hand, and we prayed together. Then we stepped outside, talking and praying for another half hour.

Taxi Needed!

As I walked back to my hotel to grab my luggage, I was overwhelmed praising God. I recalled what He had told me a year and a half ago while I was in Israel: that I would be His voice and His hands, to bless and lift up others. To think—I almost skipped breakfast! However, the talk had delayed things and now I was running late for the airport. I hurriedly packed and tried to call a taxi. After three attempts, I kept getting a message that no taxis were available. Despite this, I felt an unshakable peace and began praying for a way to get to the airport. Just then, a taxi pulled over. I ran over, and to my surprise, the car was empty, and the driver agreed to take me to the airport immediately. Once again, God had made a way.

When I arrived at the airport, I needed to put some extra items into the luggage I had placed in long-term storage at the airport the evening before, as I was not bringing that bag to

China. The staff initially refused, saying I couldn't access the bag. As I prayed silently, the attendant suddenly changed his mind — though with a frown — and handed me my bag. Another miracle.

Prayer Chapel Surprise: Donut or a Blessing?

Rushing through security, I headed to the gate. On the way, as I walked quickly, I noticed a store selling Korean souvenirs, with people dressed in traditional silk dresses and warrior outfits. The sight was a bit comical and totally distracted me. I almost missed the sign over my head that said *Prayer Chapel*. I had seen signs like that many times in airports, yet this felt different and I knew God wanted me to go to it. However, I was running late and just kept quickly walking to the gate, to hopefully eat before getting on the flight. I thankfully arrived at the gate quickly. To my surprise it was right next to the Prayer Chapel. I chuckled, what are the odds that this could happen in this huge terminal! Also, even more happily, I noticed there was a Dunkin Donuts café also next to the gate. I was hungry for a donut; so I decided to go there immediately. God nudged me thought, to go to the prayer chapel first.

Reluctantly, I entered the chapel. There was a Muslim-looking man who was putting his shoes on, getting ready to leave. He must have read my mind, because he said that this prayer room is for all religions, and that he is a Christian. I walked over to him and asked him where he was from. He said his name was Alex, and he was from Africa. I felt compelled to ask him about his story and why he was traveling to Korea. With that question, his face changed. It went from a smile, to a frown with much tiredness in his eyes. He asked me, *do you really want to know?* I said, *yes*. Alex proceeded to tell me how he had been stuck at the airport for two and a half months, a prisoner there. Unable to enter as his tourist visa had been revoked when he arrived, and he was fearful of being killed if he went back to his home country in Africa. He felt isolated, digging for food, alone at the airport, even as he walked the airport daily surrounded by thousands of people. He was a prisoner. I was shocked, my heart was moved. I had never heard of anyone who was in a situation like this. Later, I would find out he was not alone, but a few dozen men and women were in the same predicament, some for up to a year, all at that airport.

I asked if I could pray for him, and his eyes filled with tears as he eagerly said yes. So, we both knelt down together in the prayer room. With my hand on his shoulder and my other hand under his two hands, I asked for God to bless him, to set him free from this prison at the airport. That he would feel the profound love of God, and know that God sees him. I felt to pray like Moses, that God would part the Red Sea for him, that he would be able to walk through on dry land. That Alex would be molded by God through this difficult situation to be a powerful man of prayer. For him to realize this was his calling, to be a strong man of God, with his prayers impacting lives and nations, moving mountains and blessing many. At the end of praying for him, Alex turned to me with eyes wide, many tears at this point, asking me if I was a pastor. Stating no one had really talked with him in all his time here, and definitely no one had prayed for him in these last two and half months. It meant everything to him. He said there was a woman he met a few weeks ago who said she would pray for him, but she was in a hurry and didn't have time to do it at that moment. It hit me and tears formed in my eyes. All of this was happening in a country that had one of the largest percentage of Christians of any nation on Earth. Also, I had just left a conference with 5,000 Christian leaders, most of which has come through this airport both coming and going. He is a prisoner and no one had seen him or been moved to pray with him. The Bible tells us that Jesus would see people in need, feel compassion, and move toward them – and I almost prioritized a donut over this! I felt extremely blessed that God had opened my eyes, and my heart, as I had almost missed it. As I boarded the flight, Alex was there happily waving at me with a smile filling his face.

The Rest of the Story

Miraculously, I saw Alex again on my flight back from China to the U.S. We prayed together once more, and I have stayed in touch with him ever since. Alex, as of the writing of this, still remains at the airport, but he has embraced his calling as a man of prayer, excitedly telling me about how he has begun praying for others, just as I did for him.

Alex calls me *Dad*, and our relationship is an amazing blessing in my life. May God open our eyes to see the priceless value in the people around us. Many feel enslaved, imprisoned, may we proclaim freedom for the captives as we show them the love of Jesus.

Filled with compassion,
Jesus reached out his hand and touched the man.
Mark 1:40

All throughout the ministry of Jesus, it would say how He had compassion. The needs of others pierced his heart and broke it. He moved towards the person and would usually physically touch them to show them their tremendous value and worth. In this passage in the book of Mark, the man that he was touching had a contagious disease. Also, as a Jewish religious leader, they usually never touched a sick person. Yet Jesus consistently would break convention to show love, what would you do? Look at your own heart, as I had to with mine, do we care for others with this deep compassion? Very few do. May we be courageous and move toward that person in need as our heart overflows with compassion.

I was so richly blessed to meet him.
Alex was much more valuable than a donut!

Chapter 25

In China: Lost
(Day 11-continued)

Do not forget to entertain strangers.
For by so doing, some people have entertained angels
without knowing it
HEBREWS 13:2

The flight arrived in China late Sunday afternoon, and I was equipped with nothing but the address of my accommodation written in Chinese. Shortly after landing, I realized I had left my debit card at home, making it impossible to withdraw cash from an ATM. Thankfully, prior to traveling, I had felt God prompting me to bring a large amount of cash, which was unusual for me. I was grateful for listening to that nudge, as I exchanged the money for local currency. I then made my way to the taxi stand, where no one spoke English. Signs were posted, warning tourists that some taxi drivers might take advantage of them. Well, I thought to myself, they sure could take advantage of me. I don't know Chinese and I have no idea where this place is in Beijing. I showed the driver the address. He looked at it, smiled, then frowned, frowned deeper, before finally driving off. I prayed he knew where to go. In a city of over 20 million people, I had to trust him—and God. I was amazingly at peace.

Where is the Room?

After what felt like an eternity, we arrived at a massive complex made up of towering buildings, up to 10,000 people could easily live and work there in the tall 20-30 story structures.

The driver motioned for me to get out, pointing toward some buildings. With my bag in tow, I started walking, asking for directions as I passed people. Everyone spoke only Chinese, and all the signs were in Chinese. After talking to several people and receiving conflicting directions, I was getting more and more confused and kept praying. Eventually, I found a building that I just felt may be the right one, but it was locked. I had the code for the lodging door, but not for the building itself I realized. It was at this point I started to realize I was lost in Beijing and it was getting dark, a city of over 20 million people, without any way to easily get help. God brought me here, *He would have to come through.* It hit me;

I was lost in China

As I stood there praying, two people exited the towering structure, and I quickly slipped inside. The interior felt like a scene from the 1950s — dim, dusty, with a flickering light bulb near the elevator. Old bicycles and planters, seemingly untouched for decades, filled the space. Posters praising the achievements of the Communist Party adorned the walls, and everywhere I looked, there were Chinese flags celebrating the national holiday. The address I had was cryptic, mentioning the numbers two and three in the midst of all the Chinese characters, so I assumed the location might be on the third or second floor. Taking the small elevator up to the third floor, the doors had keyed locks, not the combination code that I had received.

At this point, I was becoming desperate to take care of what happens when you drink a lot of water. I hadn't used the bathroom in a long time, and I realized that if I left the building, I might not be able to get back in. In a less-than-ideal situation, let's just say I figured out a solution, making the need to find the place even more urgent. Amazingly though, I was in total peace, laughing at this crazy situation. Alone in a foreign country with no good ability to communicate or even find the right location. It was now dark outside; I was totally dependent on God for sure! God, I knew, wanted me here so it was His responsibility to figure it out. I decided to try every door in the 25-story building with the combination I had. On the second floor the light bulb went out and it was completely dark in the hall. I pulled out my disposable cell phone, only to discover it didn't even have a flashlight. Stuck in the flickering darkness, I rummaged through my bag and found my headlamp.

A Sign!

I tried the first door. The lock blinked red. Then the second door—another red blink. I prayed harder. The hall light suddenly came back on, and I saw a sign by one of the doors, then the light flickered off. For some reason, I was drawn to that sign, and struggling with my headlamp, noticing Chinese writing on it. I had seen Chinese characters all day and hadn't thought much of it, yet somehow this seemed important. This time, using a translation app on my phone, it read:

> *Do not forget to entertain strangers, for by so doing some*
> *people have entertained angels without knowing it.*
> *Hebrews 13:2*

There I stood, in a dark hallway in Beijing, staring at words about angels, my eyes open wide in surprise. Earlier this same day in Korea, during breakfast with my friend Esmael, he had mentioned that I seemed like an angel to him. Now, here I was, staring at what felt like a divine sign that I was in the right place. I re-entered the code into the lock, but it still blinked red. I tried every variation I could think of. It blinked red and started buzzing at me, not a good sign, I thought. Despite this, I felt at peace knowing I was in the right place. At that moment the elevator opened, and a young man was inside. I showed him the address, and he pointed, confirming it was the door with the angel sign by it.

Knowing now for sure it was the right location; it puzzled me why the code didn't work. It was totally dark outside, and I realized I had no way to contact anyone except by email. I sent a message explaining the situation, and after standing there for a few minutes, realized that it may be hours or days before the person would look at their email. I decided to try calling the Chinese number using my American cell phone, even though I wasn't sure it would work. Miraculously, it did, the person saying I would get the correct door code shortly. I stood there in the dim hallway, waiting, and feeling a profound sense of peace. It might take a few hours, but I knew God would come through, as He had led me this far. In just a few minutes I got the new door code. This one worked, and I was finally able to enter where I'd be staying alone for the next three days.

During my flight to Beijing, I had felt overwhelming joy from God, filling page after page of my journal. I sensed this trip wasn't about spiritual warfare or challenges but about love and claiming something very precious. A warm love, like having a child, or receiving a bride. My heart was so full of God's love and peace that it was hard to concentrate. As I settled into the room that Sunday evening, with a dinner consisting of a handful of nuts I had in my bag, I had no idea what lay ahead for the next few days. Would they be easy or incredibly difficult? Either way, I was at peace, knowing that God had been guiding me.

I slept peacefully that night in the utter quiet of the place, cut off from the world I knew, but knowing that **God was with me.**

Chapter 26

ALL of God's Love
(Day 12)

A new command I give you: Love one another.
As I have loved you, so you must love one another.
JOHN 13: 34

Tears welled up in my eyes and dripped onto the glass-topped coffee table in Beijing. God had told me to spend the last day of September and the first two days of October in prayer and fasting for the nation and people of China. So, on Monday, September 30th, I found myself alone in Beijing, fasting and praying. When someone dedicates time to God in solitude, He moves in powerful ways. Throughout the day, I felt God's presence surrounding me in the most beautiful way. I was physically alone, and my heart also felt the ache of emotional solitude — the sense that no one else could truly understand or would even desire to share in this journey, hearing and feeling my heart. Yet God comforted me. He was so real in that room, making His presence known.

Earlier that year, in February, God had given me a new heart, replacing mine with His own — a profound seven-day journey that's part of a larger story, perhaps for another book. So, I already carried God's full heart of loving mercy. There in Beijing, I asked God how He wanted me to pray, and I kept sensing the need to pray to receive *all of His love* — not just a part of it, but the fullness of God's love to utterly fill me.

This is what I wrote in my journal that day. I realize it is very personal, and parts could be misunderstood, so I had debated putting it in, but felt God desired me to include all of it in its entirety.

I feel a bit sleepy, so I lay down. You, my Master, speak. I hear You say, 'Listen today. Do not speak in prayer. Listen to My voice. I am making you Mine, My bride. You asked for all My love, and I will show you. You will be consumed by My love, just as a bride surrenders to her groom. Absolute surrender to the One you have given yourself to. My love will pierce you, penetrate into your very being. You will feel My passion for you. My seed I will plant in you, and you will bear life. I, the Lord, will guide you, lead you, love you, and protect you. You did not choose Me – I chose you. What is conceived in you is of Me. You asked for all of My love, and I will give it to you. Your greatest joy will be to please Me, just as your wife delights in pleasing you, and she will do even more. Rich blessings will cover you all your days until you are with Me. Do not fear. Victory and triumph are yours. The riches of nations will be yours, the choicest fruits given to you, for you are My bride. These are gifts to you. Your surrender to My love is My highest desire. You please Me, My faithful one. Receive My love now. Your heart is My heart. I give you the heart of a woman, added to your own. You asked, 'Why love? Why not power or wisdom?' You think you are here in China to pray? You will, but with ALL my love for the people I love. Remember, the greatest of these is love. You wisely asked for My love because I, your Groom, desire to give you all of Me. I am love. Love is patient, kind, not with envy, does not boast, not proud, not rude, not self-seeking, not easily angered, remembers no wrong, does not delight in evil, rejoices in truth, always protects, always trusts, always hopes, always perseveres. Love never fails. You are being matured to be My gorgeous bride, reflecting My love to the world. I will cover your imperfections so that the world will see My perfect love. The greatest, the GREAT path is LOVE. Love has come to China, to Tiananmen. Heaven will be torn open. My love has come. That is the seed, love, that you my vessel carry. It will be life. There will be pain in the birth, then overwhelming joy! Joy! I, the Lord, give you joy!

At that moment, suddenly the sun broke through the clouds for the first time that day. It pierced the sky, cutting through the big trees filling the room bathing me with warm, radiant light.

This discussion with God is still something I am processing through. The Bible tells us that those who believe in Him are the *Bride of Christ*, but as a man, I struggle to fully comprehend this reality of being God's bride. Women are blessed to naturally better understand this than men.

Through this, God reminded me of a promise. Back in February 2020, in Washington D.C., I was praying with my good friend Pedro from Costa Rica in front of the White House early one morning, hours before sunrise. We had asked God how we should pray, and I felt drawn to the book of Acts. Pedro immediately sensed the same and pointed to chapter one. We read together:

*… **wait** for the gift My Father promised…*
For John baptized with water, but in a few days, you will be baptized with the Holy Spirit. It is not for you to know the times or dates the Father has set by His own authority.
But you will receive power
when the Holy Spirit comes on you, and you will be My witnesses in Jerusalem, in all Judea and Samaria,
and to the ends of the earth.
(Acts 1:4-5, 7-8)

Now, here I was in China, far from home; I was literally on the other side of the world. Waiting—yes, that word *wait* that had once felt like a four-letter curse word to me. I was also receiving God's power, much differently than I expected, as that power I was learning was His love for people. As I sat there with my tears forming small puddles on the table, I realized that waiting and loving wasn't a bad thing. It was a blessing. God is faithful to His promises, just as He says in Psalm 145:13, *The Lord is faithful to all of his promises*. My faith was growing, realizing that waiting on God is a wonderful part of the journey. God and I continued this amazing dialogue throughout the day, filling more pages of my journal.

The last statement I heard Him say that day was:
As you receive My love, you will love what I love – people.
You will carry their pain, and you will love them.
This is love: that you love others as I have loved you.

My response:
Lord, please show me how much You love me,
so I may love others as You do.

His reply:
I will

I had already received Christ's heart in a miraculous way earlier in the year in a different nation, and now God was filling it with His love—a love that I came to understand was for people. God loves people. All of God's love can be summed up in one truth: *it is love for all people.* John 3:16 tells us that God sent His Son to die for the people of this world because of His great love for them. That's what His love is all about. Part of me felt excited, yet also nervous. My heart was already so full of love for people, and I knew that God was about to expand it even more.

Loving like God means Loving People.

I knew the concept in my head.
God was now transforming my heart to actually do it.

Chapter 27

Loving 1.4 billion People
(Day 13)

Above all, love each other deeply
1 PETER 4:8

I was up early that morning, out the door about 5:00 AM on October 1, 2024. I knew God wanted me in the heart of China, Tiananmen Square, on the 75th anniversary of the founding of the nation. I imagined I wouldn't be the only one with this idea.

At the modern subway, a guard helped me get a ticket since everything was in Chinese, and I couldn't navigate it myself. After a 45-minute ride, I exited near Tiananmen Square, but was unsure of the way due to the many security barriers. Smoothly, almost invisibly, I passed through three different checkpoints, where facial recognition and security cards were required. Waving my blue US passport, security just waved me past. It had taken me hours to arrive, but now I was here. The massive square was surrounded by key monuments: the National Museum of China, the entrance to the Forbidden City, Chairman Mao's mausoleum—with his embalmed body on display, and the Great Hall of the People. In the center, a huge metal sculpture of a flowerpot displayed the years *1949 to 2024* and *75th Anniversary*. Tens of thousands of people were gathered, many waving small red Chinese flags. Many women wore heart-shaped stickers of the Chinese flag on their cheeks, celebrating this national holiday.

The atmosphere was serene, peaceful and joyful—nothing like the noisy celebrations I was used to on the 4th of July back home in the USA, when the US celebrates its national anniversary as a nation. People were taking photos, and multiple people approached me, eager to practice their English or for me to hold their children for a picture. I didn't sense any fear, only quiet happiness.

As I stood before the massive flower sculpture, I felt God telling me to walk around it seven times and pray for the heavens to be torn open, for His love to pour down on China. Just as the heavens opened when Jesus was baptized, I prayed for that same love to fill the nation. The whole scene felt pure, simple, and sacred, as though God Himself was blessing the people.

> *As Jesus was coming up out of the water,*
> *he saw Heaven being torn open*
> *and the spirit descending on him like a dove.*
> *Mark 1:10*

Mission Complete: Time to Eat

After spending several hours in the square, I felt my mission was complete, and it was time to leave. I was glad I had come early because by the time I left, the crowds trying to enter were immense. God told me to break my fast that day, turning the day into a celebration. His love had descended, filling me like the joy of a wedding feast, so I found a local mall and enjoyed a hearty meal; beef and noodle soup, rice, heart-shaped egg, lemon iced tea, and the best pastries ever (I ate two, it was a time to celebrate!).

At lunch, I read where I was at in the Bible for that day,

> *The spirit of the Lord is on me, because he has anointed me to*
> *preach good news to the poor. He has sent me to proclaim*
> *wisdom for the prisoners and recovery of sight for the blind, to*
> *release the oppressed, to proclaim the year of the Lord's favor.*
> *Luke 4:18-19*

As I ate, I reflected on God's mysterious ways and how this is the perfect verse for today. It was very similar to the verse the Korean woman gave me on my first day in Asia. I did feel that the Spirit of the Lord was on me and that he has anointed me to preach good news. In this case, the good news was His love and to proclaim it over the entire nation of China. God reminding me of how approximately 25 years ago I had been in China for my first business trip. I had prayed that God would bless the Chinese people. Now, 25 years later, I was back. I was able to pray for the nation again and to see how over these 25 years China had increased in prosperity and how the people have been blessed. I was overjoyed.

Laughing at myself, I reflected on when I asked to receive all of the love of God, believing that I would feel more of his love for me. Instead though, *He increased my love for all people!* Every person I had seen today, I felt I could relate to and I loved them so much, like God does. I wanted them to be blessed, have healthy families, children, good careers, freedom, safety and to truly know how much the Lord God loves them. Even the uniformed man and woman police officers posing for a picture, then suddenly kissing. That surprised me! Only after did I realize they were a married couple. Standing there in the center of China, God expanded His love in my heart. The hundreds of people from so many nations I had just met in Korea, their names and faces also flooded my mind. I loved all of them! I was immersed in a treasure room filled with priceless masterpieces, with what God loved most, people. My eyes were opening and the joy blinded me. I had asked God, for ALL of His love, and I felt it. It did not crush me, but elated me. God's love pouring over and into me, consuming me with an overwhelming affectionate love and care for so many. I laughed at myself again, *what a mystery!* I sure did not understand all of this. I felt so satisfied and kept thanking God.

Writing in my journal to close this amazing day in the center of China, on its 75th anniversary, October 1, 2024.

Lord, your ways are a mystery! I looked at thousands of Chinese today. I just feel love. Lots of love, no animosity. The people here do not fear America. I know the Chinese people have a precious place in your heart. It feels like their leaders are looking for global respect. Lord, use me as a peacemaker. I am sorry, Lord. I now realize I did not love as you do. Thank you for giving me your earth-filling powerful overwhelming love! Lord, somehow as I am in your presence, I am your ambassador. China has been claimed with your love, and you used me as the vessel, your ambassador to do that. Amen. It was easy! No battle, all the doors opened, I walked through on a smooth path. Just like you said when I was leaving Intel the summer of 2022, that the path would be smooth. I believe it was the prayers of all my friends, the saints, that opened these doors and I just walked though on smooth ground. Lord, I look again in the Bible at Luke 4:18. It is truly your spirit that is on me. Thank you. Love has come today.

What a uniquely overwhelming day, as my heart swelled to love so many people, as it was being filled with all of God's love. What is better than this? Nothing. It was an amazing day.

As you ponder this, what does *deeply loving* look like, practically? A handshake or more of a hug? A glance, or a long look of compassionate care? A quick hello or dedicated time of seeing and hearing a person? Saying *nice to see you*, or saying *I love you*? Yes, it is likely different from what you do today and not what others do, as it should be. If you act and love exactly like those around you, you are likely not walking with God. Let me say that again:

> *If you love others like those around you do.*
> *You are likely not walking with God,*
> *but walking with the world.*

Loving others like this is radical, it is different, it takes courage. Few are on this path; I pray you choose to join me.

Peter, an apostle of Jesus and the first leader of the Church, did not have this sort of love at the beginning of his walk with God. Jesus told Peter three times right before He went to heaven to deeply love people, as obviously Peter wasn't doing that yet! However, Peter developed this profound compassionate love years later, after spending decades following God. Peter wrote with so much emphasis on love, writing how this is above all the most important thing. May we love the same way.

Above all, love each other deeply
1 PETER 4:8

Chapter 28

Merciful Love for All
(Day 14)

Loving toward all that he has made.
PSALM 145:17

I woke up early, made my way to the local grocery store, and picked up some breakfast. I love the food in China! As I sat at the kitchen table, I gazed out the window at the street below. The first light of day was beginning to edge around the buildings, though it was still mostly dark. An elderly man in his pajamas shuffles past on the street below, stopping at a row of black plastic trash cans, struggling to throw away old shoes.

As I watch him, Philippians 2:5-11 came to mind, reminding me of Jesus' life—a life devoted to serving others, humbling Himself in love. Then, my thoughts drift to John 3:16: *For God so loved the world that He gave His only Son...* I think of our two sons and am struck by the depth of God's love. Tears come again, this time pooling on the glass kitchen table. I chuckle through my tears, realizing how thoughtful God is—all the furniture is prepared for my frequent weeping! Oh, how He cares about every detail!

Writing in my journal:

Lord Jesus, I weep! My heart shaking, how You LOVE all people. Not things, but people, with all your merciful heart. You see. You grieve. So much pain in this world. I felt some of your love. Lord, may I feel it all. All please Lord! I want to know You. You are Love! To fully know you Lord, please, please show me ALL Your love. Your love is for all people I now understand. (1 John 4:8,16) May I also have all this love,

138

*for people, to know You more! That Lord means more to me,
well, I was going to say "more than healing people and
nations", but you corrected me. Your heart wants to heal
hearts, people, nations. You wait for people to desire this also,
to have Your heart. I do Lord! I have Your heart you gave to
me in Poland this year, and I desire to be Your love on earth.
To lovingly touch, heal, mend, build, align, protect and bless,
all people, all nations, those You bring to me. I will not despise
or reject, but will move toward them in merciful love. Love –
is knowing Your love, knowing You, means deep merciful
love for others. Amen.*

Later, I felt led to walk and pray near the US Embassy and
other embassies in Beijing. The streets were lined with security
cameras, and young men in masks leaned against the buildings,
watching me and the few other pedestrians intently. I felt at
peace, knowing I was following God's leading. As I walked, I
prayed, claiming the area with God's love. Afterward, I visited
a large shopping mall — empty on this holiday week except for
the many vendors that competed for my attention. I prayed for
the people I passed and made a mental note that *Hot and Sour*
soup in China is ten times spicier than in the US — it packed a
punch, pure fire. I will remember that!

Longing for Our Spiritual Family
Returning to the room, I spent more time with God,
reflecting on Philippians 3:8 and how, like Paul, I now consider
everything on this earth as of little value, compared to the
surpassing greatness of knowing God. The first verse of
Philippians 4 also resonated with me:
> *Therefore, my brothers and sisters, you whom I love and
> long for, my joy and crown, stand firm in the Lord in this
> way, dear friends!*

This perfectly captured how I was feeling — overflowing
with love and longing to be with my brothers and sisters in
Christ — as well as be reunited with my dear wife and boys.

Chapter 29

Daughter of Abraham
(Day 15)

Shouldn't this woman,
a daughter of Abraham,
...be set free on the Sabbath?
LUKE 13:16

This morning, I was reading Luke chapters 13 and 14. I began to weep again, thankful the kitchen table was covered with glass. *I am becoming a walking shower of tears*, I thought! All of this made me laugh as I ate my morning yogurt, wrote in my journal, and read the Bible. I was reading from Luke 13:10-16.

> *On a Sabbath Jesus was teaching in one of the synagogues, and a woman was there who had been crippled by a spirit for eighteen years. She was bent over and could not straighten up. When Jesus saw her, he called her forward and said, 'Woman, you are set free from your infirmity.' Then he placed his hands on her, and immediately she straightened up and praised God. The synagogue leader was indignant because Jesus had healed on the Sabbath. He said to the people, 'There are six days for work, so come and be healed on those days, not on the Sabbath.' The Lord answered, 'You hypocrites! Doesn't each of you untie your ox or donkey from the stall and lead it to water on the Sabbath? Shouldn't this woman, a* **daughter of Abraham***, whom Satan kept bound for eighteen years, be set free on the Sabbath?'"*

This passage really touched my heart. Especially the caring way Jesus called her a *daughter of Abraham*. The rest of the day I was in prayer and feeling His presence. Alone time, fully isolated with God, is amazing!

That evening, I was excited. After years of doing video calls with Maci, I finally was able to meet her, and with her was a young lady named Lily. Meeting her finally face to face, Maci and I both could not stop grinning. God answers prayer! I had shared with her over 3 years ago how I dreamed to travel to China to meet her family and see her church. She had prayed that day, asking for God to make it happen, and in a confident voice told me *Craig, it will happen. I can't wait to meet you in China.* Now that day had arrived. That evening we walked to a shopping mall and had dinner with two women who work for a large multinational company in China. They had found Christ through a small group at work, and now I had the joy of sharing a meal with them. They kept ordering more and more food, and we shared stories, laughter, and ate an amazing meal. One woman had just recently accepted Christ, while another had been a believer for 19 years but was struggling because her husband did not share her faith. After dinner, the four of us stood outside, holding hands in a circle as I prayed for each of them.

As we prayed, the young woman who had just recently received the love of God in her heart, told us with much joy how she felt as if a burden had been lifted from her shoulders. The woman about my age, with tears streaming down her face, remained silent, simply moved by God's Spirit of love for her. God calls us to love sincerely, this requires slowing down and to move toward others as Jesus did, and then there is healing. In doing so, we bless others richly, and I returned to the room full of joy, barely able to sleep. Truly, following God and serving others is the greatest path.

Do we treat women as Daughters of Abraham?

I am a father of two amazing boys. I know the intense love of a father toward a child. Yet I and every man I have talked to who has a daughter agree, in the heart of every father is an extra special place of even more love for your little girl, your daughter. While it is not explicitly stated in the Bible, I believe that as the ultimate loving Father, God feels the same way. God the Father has an especially tender love for His daughters, the precious *Daughters of Abraham*. Men especially, as we follow the ultimate man, Jesus, may we treat women this same way. All women are daughters of the King!

Ladies – you are tenderly loved by God!
You are a beloved *Daughter of Abraham*.

Chapter 30

Joy in His Presence
(Day 16)

you will fill me with joy in your presence
PSALM 16:11

Last day in Beijing, today taking a train to a different large city in China. Oh, how God's ways are perfect! The night before, I had dinner with three women – daughters of Abraham. Earlier that same day had read about how the male religious leaders resented Jesus for lovingly healing a woman, as He broke protocol. What hurt my heart was realizing that 2,000 years later, some followers of Christ, still act more like those religious leaders. They criticize and condemn, rather than showing the compassion and love of Jesus. They stick to the rules, tradition, protocol, organizational preservation, and seek job security, preferring caution with safety – relegating loving others to second priority. The Bible consistently tells us that God is love, and we repeatedly see Jesus moved by compassion; reaching out to touch physically and emotionally those in need to heal them. Yet so many of His followers don't do the same.

As I sat in Beijing, I wrote in my journal:

We don't see women for who they truly are – precious daughters of Abraham. Lord, we lack your compassion, mercy, and love. We are hypocrites! We speak of God and love, yet we fail to love those placed right beside us. We fear man and his rules more than we love God. I am sorry, Lord! Give me Your love fully, pushing out the fear of man. You led me now to Luke 14:26, reminding me that everything else must come second, even what I hold dearest, as a disciple has only

143

one Lord. I choose You, Jesus. I've given up wonderful time with my beloved wife and sons, the comfort of home, and security – having risk and loneliness as I follow... yet I am blessed! As Mark 10:29 says, you have provided for me even as I have left home. Here I am in China, staying in a place miraculously provided to me, welcomed by people from so many nations. Luke 14:33 tells me I must give up everything to be Your disciple, and looking at it now, I see what a good choice it was to follow You here.

Breakfast and Praise at a Chinese House Church

I grabbed my bag and walked out of that blessed place for the last time. I made my way through the large complex to meet two friends for breakfast at a house church that meets there. As we talked, I paced the room, then burst into singing the old hymn *Holy, Holy, Holy*, I just had to praise God! It is a song that God had placed on my heart frequently starting 8 years ago. I've been blessed to sing it and to record it with my phone in many nations and in some truly special places. Singing it in the Upper Room in Jerusalem where Jesus washed the disciples' feet, in London, Rome, Poland, and now in China, amazing! In singing, I feel it consecrates the location, claiming it with the praise of God.

> *Holy, holy, holy! Lord God Almighty!*
> *Early in the morning our song shall rise to Thee;*
> *Holy, holy, holy! merciful and mighty!*
> *God in three Persons, blessed Trinity!*
> HYMN – HOLY, HOLY, HOLY

That morning, as I sang in the house church in Beijing, Maci and Lily smiled and filmed me singing. They commented multiple times on how happy I was. I am sure they had never seen anyone early in the morning so happy and singing in the room where the church met – even without coffee! Lily was preparing breakfast in the kitchen, and it was such a joyful moment as she served us amazing food, the special Chinese egg pancakes and fruit was tasty. It felt as if heaven was slowly opening and another beautiful gift was descending. It overwhelmed me, with such raw joy! I was in Beijing, in a house church, blessing it in song and prayer and eating there with two sisters in Christ!

God had highlighted Lily to me from the moment I met her yesterday, and Maci had texted stating that she felt Lily may need prayer. Amen, I am sure this is one of the reasons God had me in China. He loves Lily as a *daughter of Abraham*, and would send me thousands of miles for her to know the love of God. I knew I'd have a chance to bless her and pray for her that morning. As breakfast wrapped up, I asked if we could all read the Bible together and pray. They both had their Chinese Bibles out, and me with my English Bible. With Maci translating, as Lily didn't speak much English, we read Psalm 145 together, I felt led to share verse 13 with her: *The Lord is faithful to all His promises and loving toward all He has made.* She started to cry. Holding her hands, I prayed for her as Maci translated, tears running down Lily's cheeks. I felt God's tender care and love for her. God's love for her overwhelmed her, and me. I was beyond blessed. A friend in China recently shared this Chinese proverb with me, and it perfectly fits.

赠人玫瑰·手留余香

*The giver of a rose
retains the lingering fragrance in their hand*

Lily had received God's love, and I could smell the sweet fragrance as God had used me to give it. Amen! She was filled, and looked a bit stunned, full of God's love that truly had sliced through the sky and filled her. Lily packed us a travel sack with enough food it seemed to feed a small nation, and gave it to us as she smiled and waved us off.

High Speed across China

Maci and I headed to the train station. During the ride, Maci shared how watching me interact and pray for others had taught her how to love more. It made my heart smile. I, in turn, was learning from her — her incredible faith and her willingness to follow God without hesitation. I had never met anyone with such confident, bold, trusting faith in God. We boarded the high-speed train, which sped smoothly at nearly 200 mph/320 km per hour, and I reflected on an earlier meeting I had after breakfast.

That morning, I met someone who had spent decades dreaming of religious freedom for China — freedom given by the government to all people in China. This new friend envisioned a law-based system versus the current bureaucracy that was overseeing religion in China. The new friend said, *to be a world leader, China must embrace freedom of religion as other nations do; the people here are crying out for it.* We had an amazing conversation by a stream in a park, and I was overwhelmed by how God was connecting me and helping me better understand the challenges and dreams of the Chinese people. With all this thinking on the train, it made me hungry, and I was thankful for the snacks Lily had packed for the train ride. It reminded me of my sweet caring wife back home, who had likely been praying for me to eat well and be taken care of. I missed my wife. I am so blessed to have a wife that so wonderfully cares for me.

> As we traveled, Maci wrote a note in my journal:
> *God is amazing! Thank you for bringing Craig to China! Thank you for all the beautiful plans to love us! From Craig, I learned how to love more, love with my whole heart. Thank you, Craig, for coming from so far away to teach me how to love others, how to pray everywhere and pray for everything. It's the most beautiful blessing to be connected with each other in His amazing love. Love never fails!*

It felt miraculous how God had brought us together. About four years ago, a friend, Mario and I had been praying for connections with Christian leaders at sites around the world. As we kept praying God worked, with the Intel Christian Employee Resource Group (ERG) growing from 3 countries to 23 nations as of 2024. Maci and I first connected in 2021 during a tough time in her life, and I had the chance to prayerfully encourage her. Now, here we were, in China on a high-speed train going to visit her family and the house church. I had shared with her my desires and prayers about coming to China, we had prayed — and here I was, a testament to the power of prayer.

Hearing God once Changed His Life

After arriving, I met Maci's family and the house church community, including the Pastor. That evening, after a huge meal prepared by Maci's husband, I had a conversation with the pastor with Maci translating. I wanted to tell him how God had led me here, but that did not occur, he needed me to see him, listen, care and to pray. He shared his story of struggle, how he had powerfully heard God's voice once in his life, leading him to leave a large church in a large city to pastor a small church for university students in Beijing. His decision to follow God caused him incredible hardship; including criticism from his former Pastor, those he had gone to seminary with, and others. Then after moving, his new church had dwindled to just two members. He and his family barely had enough food, with he and his wife taking turns on who would eat dinner each night. Yet, they kept following God on this path He had called them to. Now he has started and leads a dozen house churches in different cities. He also showed me several devotional books he had written on the Bible — one chapter for each chapter of scripture; there were five books! His vision was to help others in China, especially leaders, truly understand the Bible. However, due to restrictions on religious literature sales in China, he had to raise money to print and donate these books.

Moved by his story, I asked if he could put his hand on the books, I placed my hand on top of his hand and prayed. Maci was there translating for us. God had used me to focus on him, to see, listen, and to lift up my dear brother in prayer. It reminded me again how everyone needs to be seen, heard and loved - with prayer being a tender loving way to show the love of God. God was using me, and I was in awe of how He had brought me here to China to bless a pastor of a network of over a dozen house churches.

On the Floor, Filled with Joy!

That night, I slept on the floor in the basement of the house church. As I read my Bible, John 1:16 stood out to me:

From the fullness of His grace,
we have all received one blessing after another.

It perfectly described how I felt. Lying there in China, in a house church on the floor, I was overwhelmed with blessing after blessing, flooded with JOY! An amazing day and evening! As I was in the basement; there was absolute silence. In the quiet of that space, God's presence enveloped me in a sense of peace and soaking blessing. I was with Him; He was with me, I was complete.

Psalm 16:11 echoed in my heart:

> *You have made known to me the path of life;*
> *you will fill me with joy in your presence,*
> *with eternal pleasures at your right hand.*

I was in His presence. I had joy.

Do you feel joy?
Seek to be in His presence.
Loving others and praising God,
are great ways to enter into His presence.

Chapter 31

We are Connected
(Day 17)

From Him the whole body,
joined and held together by every supporting ligament,
grows and builds itself up in love,
as each part does its work.
EPHESIANS 4:16

Woke up at 5:00 AM, eager to have some quiet time alone before the day's events unfolded. The church service wouldn't start for a few hours. It was Saturday, and I later learned that the group holds services on Saturdays so that members can spend all Sunday — as their Sabbath — all together as a church family resting and having fun. Wow! In the USA and in all countries I have been to, after church families go home. At this church they spend one full day, Sunday, all together.

I sat on a piano bench in the basement by the window, in the very spot where about 15 people would soon gather for church. Although I knew God was with me, I still felt lonely. I longed to share this incredible moment with someone, a close friend, a person. A heart-to-heart friend that I would be able to share all of this with. I prayed to God, and his response was quite simple saying *no doubt.* I thought, *I will look to you Lord to provide someone that I can run this race with, as I so much desire. I will wait.* God spoke again, saying just one word, *Enjoy!*

That word was significant. A year and a half earlier, while I was in Israel, I had similar feelings of loneliness. I was surrounded by people, yet none truly understood, or desired to understand my heart. In that moment, God had spoken the

149

same word to me. I was staying at a resort by the Dead Sea, sitting by the pool. I was praying and crying out to God for direction, He whispered just one word, *Enjoy!* I was amazed, and confused by that word, and I asked Him if I had heard correctly. As I asked, I opened my eyes and looked up, about 15 stories up at the top of the large hotel, I saw the word *ENJOY* written in huge 20-foot-high capital letters on the side of the building. God totally has a sense of humor! I am sure that in this moment all of heaven was laughing and congratulating God how He could communicate to me in such an unexpected way. Here in China, God was reminding me once again to ENJOY. I couldn't help but chuckle thinking, *would God also write ENJOY in large letters on some building or structure here in China?* That morning, I had been reading in John 2, how Jesus' first miracle was also to help people enjoy life more by turning water to wine. It always makes me smile how God orchestrates what I read in the Bible to the daily lesson He wants to teach me.

Pain in Following

I wrote in my journal about how I felt alone, even with many people around me in this location and globally. All of this helping me to understand a little of what Paul the Apostle must have felt, as written in 1 Corinthians 12:1,4 stating:

> ...*visions and revelations from the Lord...*
> *heard inexpressible things,*
> *things that man is not permitted to tell.*

I sensed God was using this as part of His plan, His will, to have ongoing pain in my life. To keep me humble and to soften my heart so I could better empathize with others. I felt Him telling me that He may never take this pain of feeling alone fully away, and that I should not fear. It was hard to hear all this, but I knew I could trust Him. He was also showing me that no single person could meet all my diverse needs — only the full Body of Christ could satisfy that, with my wife and family playing their core central part. This being revealed felt like a foretaste, a savor of heaven, a deep connection to all of His Body, His children, with my dear wife and children there in the center. We are all connected, and I needed to learn that—to lean on the rest of God's Body. *(Note-Appendix B in the back has a related poem)* I was hoping for an easy answer, but I began to realize that this was part of the mystery of God's ways, and God was giving me a peek, opening my eyes. I was richly blessed, even as my heart hurt, longing for heaven when I will be fully united with God and His Body. This mixture of pain commingled with overflowing blessing and joy I would realize is part of the journey as we follow Him.

Pain commingled with Joy

As I continued reading in that quiet room where the church service would be, I read John 4:13, where Jesus speaks to the Samaritan woman about Him being the water of life. His love, He said, would well up inside of believers and overflow, gushing out to touch the lives of others. I marveled at how Jesus broke cultural barriers to have this conversation with her, and how His message of love still resonates today.

Chinese House Church Service

The service that morning was with 10 adults and a few kids. Maci, played the piano while her husband Christopher played guitar. Two other women joined them in singing up front, all dressed in green choir robes, happily singing in Chinese and smiling. The Pastor wore a suit, and a table was set with a beautiful white silk cloth adorned with a large red cross with embroidered Chinese characters. The sermon, in Chinese, was based on Genesis 1, specifically about the Spirit of God hovering over the waters—interestingly, I had just been reading about Jesus as the water of life that very morning! As I couldn't understand the rest of the service, I looked through John for other times Jesus talks about water, coming to John 7:38.

Whoever believes in me as the scripture has said,
streams of living water will flow from within him.

As I sat in this beautiful Chinese church service, meeting in the basement of a 30-story building, I felt such unity with my brothers and sisters. I thought about this verse and the streams of living water flowing from within. God was reminding me of the prayers others had spoken over me. I recalled three different people from three different countries — Romania, Jamaica, and Poland — who, at different times this year, had prayed and seen the same thing: that God was creating in me an everlasting fountain, a waterfall of His love, pouring out onto others. My heart was filled with excitement, feeling that God was speaking directly to me. I had been pouring out His love into people, and it felt like I truly had this stream of living water flowing in my life. Just like the verse says, it's because I believe in Him, and believing requires following as it tells us in James 2:17:

Faith by itself, if it is not accompanied by action, is dead.

It's so simple — we need to believe then just follow Him — and it results in streams of living water blessing everyone around us.

During that moment, I used a translation app on my phone to understand more of what was being said around me. They were talking about 2025 goals, and I felt God impress upon me three specific things He wanted me to do:

- Write a book, before 2025 begins.
- Spend even more time daily with God.
- Date my wife more intentionally.

The Love I Give, Reflects the Worth I Assign

Even though I was surrounded by people speaking a different language, I felt alone with the Lord. God opened my eyes to a profound truth: the amount of love I have for someone or something is directly proportional to the value I assign. Whether it's my wife, a car, pizza, or a stranger in need,

the love I give, reflects the worth I assign

What is the value I give to people? **What are people worth?** God reminded me of His immense love for us — so great that He sent His Son to die for us. His love for people is beyond comprehension, and it's this merciful heart of Jesus that God has placed within me, and desires to put into all of us. Now, I could expect to see people through His eyes, recognizing their immense worth and experiencing His overwhelming love for them. To God, people are worth more than even the life of His son. As a father of two sons, I could not understand that sort of value God placed on all people. That is extravagant worth!

As the Pastor transitioned into the Lord's Supper, I shared communion with my brothers and sisters in China. Communion is meant to unite the Body of Christ as it clearly tells us in 1 Corinthians 11. Yet, depending on the Christian tradition, it often does not unite but divides. Some groups do not allow brothers and sisters to participate if they are part of a different Christian tradition. This grieves the heart of God. Jesus foresaw this coming, and prayed against it in His prayer for unity in John 17. Here in China in the basement with my dear brothers and sisters it was truly priceless and united us as one Body. After the service, most people went upstairs to eat, but a few remained in the basement with me. God highlighted two women to me. I began speaking with one of them, her name was Angel. She opened up about the loss of her father the previous year and how she had recently accepted Christ. Her father's death had devastated her; he had been her loving support. She had no sibling, no mother, and she felt lost, even questioning the purpose of life. Angel had sought help from a hospital due to her ongoing depression. With tearful eyes, she shared her pain.

Let's pause here: Is this a normal conversation?

Look at what's happening. This isn't a normal conversation. Suddenly meeting a stranger and talking about deeply personal things, including the death of your father. Yet, this has happened constantly, as you have read. This kind of close sharing happens so often it is normal, I expect it, and it is wonderful to go there. How does someone open up so quickly to a complete stranger? I can only say it's God working, the Holy Spirit connecting people, allowing them to feel His love and care. It is not me; it is all God flowing through me, a weak human, and people see the love of God. Over time, I've come to see these moments as a glimpse into the greatest treasures of heaven. God allowing a quick glance at the masterpiece He has created in each person, their heart, their soul, the eternal gloriously beautiful part of their being. These conversations are like receiving precious treasures from God's throne room, each one reflecting His glory.

Compassion and Love like Jesus

A few months earlier, my own father had passed away unexpectedly, so I could highly relate to Angel's pain. It is amazing how God sent me, someone who also had just lost their own father, to minister to her. I asked if I could pray for her, and we sat down on the folding chairs where the service had been held just moments before. As I prayed, her friend Lia watched us closely. We prayed for a long time, and when I finished, Angel sat quietly for a long while, soaking in the love of Christ. Tears flowed, and she shared that she felt comforted, like something had shifted inside her — she felt loved and for the first time I saw a huge smile beaming at me. Amen!

Since that day, Angel and I have been meeting weekly over video for Bible studies, slowly reading through the book of John. She told me that after our encounter in China, she suddenly had a desire to read the Bible and had completed reading the entire Gospel of John. As we go through the verses together, she's learning that *quality is better than quantity*. Just this morning as writing this, at my 6 AM and her 9 PM, we talked about how to pray using the A.C.T.S. method (Adoration, Confession, Thanksgiving, Supplication). She was amazed that prayer was more than just asking for things. When we finished the confession part, on this particular morning, she said she felt lighter, more at peace.

During the Bible study, we read John 3:15, where Jesus says, *Everyone who believes in him may have eternal life.* Angel admitted that believing in anything eternal felt foreign to her. I didn't have a great answer at that moment, but after praying later, I felt God gave me a helpful analogy. I told her the next week. Angel believed I was in my home office in Phoenix, Arizona, in the USA, as I had told her that is where I was. She has never left China or been to the US. I asked her why she believed I was in Phoenix, even though she had no direct proof. She replied that it's simply because she trusts me. In the same way, believing in eternal life requires trust in God. This trust develops as we get to know Him, that is why prayer, listening to God and reading the Bible and other things are so important. Angel smiled, she fully understood, and then we moved on to talk about John 3:16, and it ended in a long prayer time. Beautiful, with her sitting there silently, as she was just soaking in the reality of how much God her Father loves her.

Many Questions

After talking and praying with Angel, Lia approached me with many questions. She had learned a lot about Jesus over the past few months but wasn't sure if she could trust and follow Him. She was amazed, having watched the prayer time with Angel, as she had seen Angel be transformed and now full of peace. That Saturday and Sunday Lia and I spoke a lot about faith and trust. Lia, a professional working at a large company and a mother of a 4-year-old boy, shared that she struggled to trust God. As our entire church group walked together coming back from the beach, she said, *I've never had such an open conversation like this before. I don't feel I can talk like this with others.* She admitted that sometimes she tries to just fit in, as she didn't want to feel left out. She is unsure if she can truly trust God or if He really loves her. In my mind I was praying I could talk to Lia more. God would answer that request in a special way.

As I lay down to sleep that night, I felt God speaking to me again. Maybe it had something to do with sleeping on the floor! I laughed inwardly, thinking of my son's comment earlier in the year: *Dad, do you hear that thunder? That's all the angels laughing at you!* In that moment, I felt God's love, blessing and joy pouring into me, and He said, *Enjoy, receive this blessing, feel deeply, receive all my love Craig, I love you. Receive, as I the Lord, chose on whom to bestow my riches, I have chosen you, my son. Enjoy. Receive, the riches of Heaven, all my love.*

Thank you, Lord, **I ENJOY being connected to Your Body!**

Chapter 32

A Gift and Tour of Heaven
(Day 18)

For we walk by faith, not by sight.
2 CORINTHIANS 5:7

It was Sunday morning when Maci, her husband Christopher, their two boys, and Angel—the woman I had prayed with the day before—took me shopping for my wife. Before we headed out, I was invited to Christopher and Maci's home for breakfast. I felt God wanted me to bring them the gifts I carried from the USA, so I did. I was disappointed though, as it was not the right timing to give them the gifts with the children running around. So, I left them in the corner wondering why God had me bring them that morning. Maci had prepared a traditional Chinese breakfast, and I enjoyed everything, except I just could not eat one dish: fried crickets. I just couldn't bring myself to eat them, worried that it would not end well. At the end of breakfast, Christopher leaned over and whispered to me, while Maci was in the kitchen, *I don't eat them either.* Whew!

Shopping with a Daughter

After breakfast, we piled into their new Toyota minivan and drove to the mall on a beautiful new freeway, surrounded by sleek cars. As we cruised along, I noticed a large Chinese banner on a bridge over the freeway with the word *INJOY* written in large letters next to a host of smaller Chinese characters. What!?!? I couldn't make out the rest of the message as it was all in Chinese. Almost crying, I laughed and laughed as we drove, marveling at how God loves to surprise us. I tried to explain to

156

them why I was laughing; they did not understand but smiled politely. In my mind I reflected on how God had told me to ENJOY yesterday, and today I did see a large banner! God was clearly reminding me to INJOY the day!

At the mall, Angel, who works as a professional buyer, helped negotiate everything I wanted to buy for my wife; cutting down the prices of the silk scarf, cup, and other items. The six of us ate an incredible variety of food, from pastries, to squid, to chicken, the Chinese love to eat! After all the shopping, we were walking to the car, and Angel suddenly turned to me and said *thanks Dad* with a huge smile. I looked at her and said *thanks daughter*. We both smiled, had a quick hug, then piled into the minivan with everyone. In my family, my wife and I have two wonderful boys, but God knows how I have always wanted a daughter. Part of it, I am sure, is because I observed the wonderfully impactful father/daughter relationship my wife had with her own dad, who tragically died over 20 years ago. Cesar was an amazing father (and father-in-law!) who I greatly admire. As her husband I reap the rich fruits of nurturing and protective love he planted into his little girl. It helped form her into the priceless, beautiful woman and bride she is today. In these last couple of years, God in his mysterious way, has called me to bless a number of young ladies from different countries, treating them as daughters. Today I received a Chinese daughter! What a gift, I do INJOY having a Chinese daughter!

Walking by Faith

We all drove to a park where Maci and Christopher had gotten married over 10 years ago. As we walked along the same path they had taken on her wedding day, she shared stories of her faith journey. She told about how God had called her to start an Alpha course that gives people an overview of the Christian faith, over a decade ago. The result was that over 120 of her colleagues at work had come to know Jesus. More recently, God had asked her to start a house church, which she did, and it had just opened a month before my visit. *(Note – as of this writing, a few months later, they have already grown and are preparing to create a second house church!)* I asked her how she followed God so closely, she laughed, saying that since she has no sense of direction she just has to follow. She has learned to rely completely on Him, stating:

When God says move left, I move left.
When He says move right, I move right.
I know I do not know the right direction,
but He does, so I just follow.

She mentioned that she tries to spend 30 minutes three times a day with God – morning, noon and night. In these times she is silent in His presence, or at times has light instrumental music playing, just listening to God for guidance. Her unwavering faith and desire to follow inspired me.

That evening, we met the rest of the house church at the beach. Lia continued asking me many questions about God and the purpose of life, as we skipped stones on the water with her four-year-old busy exploring the beach. I marveled at how calm, safe, and clean everything was, with Chinese families everywhere enjoying their Sunday at the beach.

Afterward, the whole group went out for dinner, where plate after plate of delicious food kept arriving. Later, Christopher and Maci drove me back. God worked a miracle, as their children went with the Pastor to where he was staying, so it was just the three of us alone in their apartment. I was thankful I had listened to God's leading to bring the gifts that morning. At their home, I gave gifts from my wife and I, including a Bible and a cross, which they truly appreciated. Hugging the gifts and holding them close to their chests.

Anointed and Seeing Heaven

Before leaving, I asked if I could pray for them and anoint them with oil I had brought from Jerusalem, where I had visited the summer before. They eagerly agreed, and with huge smiles, they sat on the couch next to each other. First, I knelt before Christopher and felt God wanted me to pray for power in his hands. I held his hands and prayed, anointing them, that he would have great power to protect Maci and open doors for them to walk through. Then I knelt before Maci, and felt God wanted me to anoint and pray for her feet. As I anointed her feet, I prayed that they would be led by God both inside and outside of China on a stable and firm path, that she would be a fragrant flower and be protected by her husband.

When we finished praying, they sat there holding hands on the couch, soaking in what had just occurred. They were silent for what seemed like a long time, both just looking at me. After a few minutes, with much curiosity, I asked Christopher how he felt, and he said simply, *powerful!* I then asked Maci, and with a serene smile, she said,

I feel like I just took a tour of Heaven.
I feel so much love.
Thank you for coming and blessing us.
You are an angel.

Amen! God's word is true. Just over a year ago, in June 2023 in Israel where I had purchased the anointing oil, I had asked God to use my life to bless others, and He had said He would. Here I was in China, blessing this dear couple I loved so much, with oil from Jerusalem. God is faithful to all of His promises, and loving toward all He has made.

May we be God's blessing to others.
Then, they can take a tour of heaven!

For where two or three come together in my name,
there am I with them.
MATTHEW 18:20

Chapter 33

Child of the King
(Day 19)

Now because you are his children,
God has sent the Spirit of his Son into our hearts
to cry out, "Abba! Father!"
GALATIANS 4:6

Up early again and spent a wonderful time with God, sitting on the piano bench in the basement, where the church service had been held. In my journal, I wrote:

Last full day here in China. Wow. Lord, I feel You are teaching me to wait, to follow, to love deeply the one sheep, enjoy, be content, and to be filled with Your love — a love for all people. You want me to see each person as a priceless, precious creation, a work of art. You've entrusted me with many, with millions, and You've entrusted me with Your dear daughters. So many are women — feeling like outcasts, not seen by others, longing to be seen and loved. To these, Lord, You have called me. The orphans, the rejected, I follow You with joy. I cherish these precious lambs.

I felt God speaking to me, saying,

I entrust My precious, needy lambs to your care.
Craig, you see how you bless? Are you content?

I reflected and summarized my thoughts to God, saying,

Yes. You are teaching me to follow, just to follow. It is the great path, the path of Abraham. Yes, Lord, I am content with just following.

I smiled, realizing God was shaping me to be like Abraham, just as He had promised seven years ago when He called me to walk by faith, not by sight, fully trusting Him on this great path. His promises always come true, even though the waiting is hard at times! As I thought through the promises God had made, I recalled some, including that He said I would support those close to the President of the United States, speak to kings and princes, lead chosen followers from many nations, and heal and bless many globally with Him flowing through my voice and hands. God also had promised close relational and physical blessings, financial provision, and protection. I was filled with joy as I reflected on all of this early in the morning on this last day in China. Realizing again how faithful God is to His promises, even when things don't happen as quickly or as I expect.

Later that day, we went to a different shopping mall where I met an artist who made paintings with the word *LOVE* in beautiful Chinese calligraphy; one of these now hangs in my home office. We ate another incredible meal, but after an hour of conversation only in Chinese, I got bored and went for a walk with Maci. While shopping, I found a huge fluffy stuffed animal that I just had to buy for my wife. Maci had watched me talk about and shop for my wife so much, she insisted on making a video—of her telling my wife what a great husband I was, as I was always buying gifts for my wife. Of course, I agreed to film it! So, I filmed Maci talking to my wife on a video in the mall.

His Daughter

As the day was ending, I had one last chance to talk with Lia. We found a small tea shop, but there were no available tables. She didn't know what to do, I prayed out loud standing next to her, asking God for a table to open up. Within ten seconds a table did! Amen! We sat down, and as we spoke, she continued to ask questions about God. We were late to go back to the group, so I asked how I could pray for her. She hesitated, then with tears in her eyes, said,

> *I want to feel and hear that God loves me,*
> *and I want to be His daughter.*

I held her hands gently, and I had the incredible joy of leading her in a prayer to become His daughter. There in that Chinese tea shop, in a mall in China, Lia received Jesus as her Father. She became His daughter that afternoon, and her face beamed with joy.

I was sitting next to a daughter of the King!

In the beautiful verse in Romans 8:15, and also in Galatians 4:6, God says when we receive Him, we call him our *Daddy.* It says, *Now because you are his children, God has sent the Spirit of his Son into our hearts to cry out, "Abba! Father!".* A few years prior when visiting Israel, I saw a young girl walking through the restaurant, lost, not knowing where her dad was, she was crying out - *Abba! Abba!* Lia was a daughter of God, she now can call Him Daddy, Abba!

There was such peace and relief on her face, the anxiety of a few minutes ago was erased, as she had taken that step to trust in Jesus. I couldn't stop smiling. It had taken her courage, stepping out in faith and taking the extended hand of God, trusting Him, even with questions remaining. As I said *Amen,* my phone rang, startling me, the call reminded us it was time to meet the group—God's perfect timing again.

A week later, Maci emailed me to say that Lia was a different person—at peace and eager to read the Bible and pray. Amen! I had been blessed to witness the transformation of Lia into a daughter of the King. It was a treasure from heaven!

Being His Light

This was also the last day I would have to talk to Maci. She told me as we left the shopping mall, *You are an angel from God. I can see the wings and the loving heart of Jesus in you.* Coming from her—a mature amazing follower of Jesus with such faith—this was the highest compliment, that I was reflecting God. Maci then shared that her husband, Christopher, would be taking me to the airport the next day, as he was eager to talk with me. It would be a wonderful opportunity to encourage him and get to know him more.

Later, I checked my phone and saw a message from Angel. She had placed the small rock I had given her on her desk at work, with a note saying it symbolized God's love for her, sent through a man from the USA. My heart was full, God had used me. There is nothing better than being used by God to bless someone!

That evening, I had a special conversation with the Pastor while Maci translated. As we spoke, I felt led to take out my Bible, and I began flipping through its pages, where I had taken many notes filling the pages with my writing. The Pastor watched me closely and finally said, after seeing my Bible, he was sure I believed in its teachings. He shared how in China, some pastors rarely use the Bible, which can lead to teachings that are not aligned to God's Word. Now that I had his confidence, we moved into a time of prayer for him and his wife. It was a priceless moment, and as we all held hands, I was blessed to pray for a pastor who leads many house churches. I kept receiving the rich treasures from heaven!

The Gift to Dream

Before leaving, Maci gave me three meaningful gifts. The first was a tapestry with the Star of David and a verse about praying for the peace of Jerusalem, which she had held onto for over a year. Amazingly, she gave it to me on October 7, exactly one year after the tragic massacre in southern Israel in 2023. The second gift was fragrant oil called *Dream* and as she gave it to me, I felt the Holy Spirit say, *this dream to support the President will happen.* Maci confirmed this even as this thought was going through my mind saying, *the dream God has given you will happen.* The final gift was a glass plate inscribed with the words, *Love never fails.* Perfect timing, I thought, as that is exactly what God has been teaching me, how love is so important. I was in awe again, all three of the gifts I felt came directly from God.

Another day filled with joy, and feeling completely overwhelmed at how God had blessed.

Chapter 34

He will Protect
(Day 20)

*He will cover you with his feathers
and under His wings you will find refuge.*
PSALM 91:4

As it was my last day I took a morning walk alone, close to where I was staying, and sang the hymn *Holy, Holy, Holy* in a large deserted shopping area, as stores had not opened yet. All of this gave me more time to pray for China and praise God for being here. Then it was breakfast time with Christopher. During our time together, Christopher and I had a wonderful conversation about purpose and God's calling. I was able to encourage him and we prayed together at the breakfast table. When we finished, he looked at me and smiled, reminding me of how rare it is for brothers and sisters in Christ to take time to truly listen and pray for each other. Breakfast and prayer – nothing better than that!

Hidden

Christopher drove me to the airport for the flight from China to Korea, and I made it to the gate quickly. However, I couldn't shake a strange feeling. There were three lines of passengers being queued to get on the flight. In one line was just myself and an American woman. In the other two lines were all the other passengers, either Korean or Chinese. There was something just not normal with this I felt. As always, I like to meet people so I was chatting with the young lady from the US who was standing next to me, as I looked around. Across the counter, by the gate, a man in a suit, with an identity badge, was watching us and everything closely. He was very serious. He seemed to have unrestricted access, as he walked anywhere he wanted. I felt compelled to pray, and as I silently did, I sensed God sheltering me under His wings, reassuring me that everything would be alright.

We finally boarded the plane, but there was a long delay before takeoff, which motivated me to pray more. Once we were in the air, I breathed a sigh of relief, knowing I was on my way to spend a night in Korea before the long flight home. During the flight to Seoul, I reflected on my week in China and how blessed I felt. I was so grateful I had obeyed God's prompting to go early to China. It felt as though my family had multiplied a hundredfold, and my ability to hear God's voice had increased in the same way. I was called, chosen, and abundantly blessed by God. He had protected me throughout the trip in China, and I had walked in peace and safety.

God does protect and shelter us, as we INJOY!

He who dwells in the shelter of the Most High will rest in the shadow of the Almighty. I will say of the Lord, "He is my refuge and my fortress, my God in whom I trust"
PSALM 91:1-2

Chapter 35

Always Ready
(Day 21)

*Preach the word; be prepared in season and out of
season; correct, rebuke and encourage — with great
patience and careful instruction.*
2 TIMOTHY 4:2

Today I was leaving Korea, and returning home to Phoenix,
Arizona, in the USA. I prayed for God to grant me divine
encounters. He certainly answered.

The morning was peaceful, and soon I was on my way to the
airport. Seoul's airport has two main terminals, and I was happy
to learn that I would be departing from the same terminal where
Alex — the man trapped at the airport — was staying. I texted him
my gate number, and he said he'd rush over to meet me. When
I saw him approaching, he had a big smile on his face. We
hugged, and I bought him lunch as we caught up.

Alex had been stuck in the airport for almost three months.
He shared how every day was a struggle to find food, and how
loneliness often weighed on him. I felt God moving through me
to remind him of his true identity. I told Alex that God had
chosen him for a special task — to learn how to pray. His painful
experience at the airport was not without purpose. It was
drawing him closer to God, preparing him to be a blessing to
others through prayer. I encouraged him that he was a warrior
called by God, destined to walk with Him, hear His voice, and
through his prayers, see lives and nations transformed.

As we spoke, his smile slowly turned to tears, overwhelmed
with emotion. He kept asking, *Are you a pastor? A preacher? Who*

are you, man of God? I smiled and said, *I am just a man who loves Jesus and people. God sent me to pray for you Alex. God loves you so much that He sent me all the way from the U.S. just to show you how important you are to Him.* He gave me a tight hug, calling me *Dad*, with tears streaming down his face. As I boarded my flight, Alex waved at me like a son watching his father leave. I was moved, amazed at how God had brought us together twice.

In the following weeks after returning home, Alex and I have stayed in touch. We text several times a week, exchanging audio messages and prayers. He calls me *Dad*, and I call him my brother and son. He has been imitating what I had done for him — praying for others he meets at the airport. I was amazed, and it reminded me of how we are to live being an example to others that they should imitate, as Paul the Apostle said in 1 Corinthians 4:16, *Therefore I urge you to imitate me.*

After I had returned home from Asia, I left him an audio prayer, asking God to guide him to someone he could meet and pray for. The next day, Alex sent me an excited audio message back. While searching for food at the airport, he approached a man who looked downcast. The man was an American, on his way to Hawaii for major surgery. Alex offered to pray for him, and the man agreed. He prayed for peace, healing, and joy. Afterward, Alex sent me a selfie of them both, their faces both glowed with happiness. Alex shared that he had gone to the man hungry, but after praying for him, he felt full of joy, no longer concerned about food. This reminded me of how Jesus responded to His followers. They had asked Him if He was hungry and Jesus replied in John 4:34, saying, *My food is to do the will of him who sent me and to finish his work.* Like Alex, when we do His will, it fills us!

Alex's situation is heartbreaking — trapped in the airport with about 40 others, afraid to return to their home countries, which are all in the greater Africa area. These people are like prisoners, and it broke my heart. I pray that God would use me in some way to help Alex and those stuck with him. Alex was my first divine encounter that day, but there was a second one waiting for me on the flight.

God talk at 35,000 feet

As I settled into my seat, one of the flight attendants caught my eye. His name was Sam, I would learn, he wore unique colorful glasses. It was clear he was a senior member of the crew. After I thanked him for something, I am not sure how, but we struck up a conversation and he opened up. He mentioned how much the world needed love and how he rarely found people who cared to talk about it. He said, *Once the flight is in the air, we need to talk more.*

Several hours into the long trans-Pacific flight, Sam tapped me on the shoulder and motioned for me to join him in the hallway. I pray for people all the time as you have noticed, but this just completely felt different. As I was walking to talk with him in the middle of the plane, I felt uneasy for some reason, so I prayed for God's wisdom and protection. We spoke for nearly an hour, and though I worried he might get in trouble for talking so long, he assured me he wanted to keep talking. He shared his thoughts about how the world lacked love, and how he saw the American culture as toxic and divisive compared to all the other countries he visits as a flight attendant. Also stating how he believed in some divine force outside of our planet or extraterrestrial creatures that had come to earth to teach us things. I, in turn, shared how God had come to earth, as Jesus, to show us God's love. Explaining that the entire message of the Bible is about God's love for humanity and how God loves him so much and wants to have a relationship with him.

At 35,000 feet, I asked Sam if I could pray for him. There, in the hallway of the large jet leaning against the exit door, I prayed. That he would feel in his heart the profound love of God for him, and that his life would be richly blessed. When we finished, his eyes were filled with tears, and he smiled. It was obvious this was a special experience for him, as it was for me. The verses from 2 Corinthians 2:14-16 came to mind: *Through us, spreads everywhere the fragrance of the knowledge of Him... to the one we are the smell of death; to the other, the fragrance of life.* Others can smell the fragrance of God in our life as we follow Him!

Sam had a sensitive spirit, and he could sense the aroma of Christ in me and in our conversation. He desired to talk to me, and God spoke His life and love into his heart. It was clear that some of the racial bitterness he carried as a dark-skinned man was being healed as I, a light-skinned man, showed him such care and prayed for him. I am thankful God allowed me to meet Sam.

Home!

I arrived home in Phoenix the same day I had left Korea, thanks to the time zone difference. Though exhausted, I was overjoyed to see my beautiful wife, dressed in a black bird-of-paradise dress, smiling and waving a small American flag. Our two boys grinned as they hugged me at the airport. That evening, we enjoyed a wonderful dinner together, and I reflected on how blessed I was to have my family that I had missed so much. My wife immersed me in her abundant love, in a joyous welcome home. Three weeks earlier, I had left nervously, with my wife in tears, missing me. Now, I was back, my heart overflowing with joy, knowing God's ways are mysterious and very good.

I will never understand His ways, so thankfully I just walk next to Him, it is truly the GREAT path, walking with God.

Chapter 36

God Rested
(Day 22-23)

By the seventh day God had finished the work
he had been doing; so, on the seventh day
he rested from all his work.
GENESIS 2:2

Rest. Sleeping for 14 glorious hours two days in a row — what a gift! After three weeks of short nights and high energy, my body craved a lot of rest, and I gladly gave in. In the few waking hours, I found myself reflecting on the trip and these powerful words from 1 Corinthians 13:13: *...the greatest of these is love.* The Bible speaks of love so often — so simple, yet so easy for me and followers of Jesus to overlook when it comes to those right in front of us.

During these past three weeks, God transformed me. This journey of simply following Him has grown more mysterious and more glorious with every step. Now, in these quiet days of rest, I sense God's call to write a book — something I have never done before, but I felt committed to completing it by the end of the year.

Chapter 37

Loving Heart or Pleasing Man
(Day 24)

*I know that you do not have
the love of God in your hearts.*
JOHN 5:42

During my quiet time with God, I was continuing the study of the book of John in the mornings, and this particular day, I found myself spending hours with God. Though I began with the book of John, God soon led me to explore many other passages, as if on a treasure hunt, as I jumped around my Bible. The words of Jesus stood out to me. They were strong and critical of the knowledgeable religious leaders of His time. Over the past few years, I had encountered many believers in Jesus — most were kind, but few were truly overflowing with love and care for others. I reflected on these verses in John 5:37-44 addressed to the leaders that know scripture.

And the Father who sent me has himself testified concerning me. You have never heard his voice nor seen his form, nor does his word dwell in you, for you do not believe the one he sent. You study the Scriptures diligently because you think that in them you have eternal life. These are the very Scriptures that testify about me, yet you refuse to come to me to have life. I do not accept glory from human beings, but I know you.

*I know that **you do not have the love of God in your hearts.** I have come in my Father's name, and you do not accept me; but if someone else comes in his own name, you will accept him. **How can you believe since you accept*** *glory from one another but do not seek the glory that comes from the only God.*

Jesus tells us very bluntly that we will struggle to believe in Him, know Him, and have His love – if we prefer the praises and glory from people more than praise and glory from God. I had been learning how God's highest desire is that we love others.

What I had observed in Korea, China and in Poland, Rome, Israel and in so many conferences as I traveled the globe, felt similar to what Jesus saw 2000 years ago. Jesus was addressing people who knew the Scriptures well, were leaders, were good people, yet missed the heart of God. They were more concerned with appearing righteous to others than with truly knowing and obeying God, where God's direct mandate is to love people. Jesus' new command wasn't to learn the Bible better, avoid sinning more, or even to pray more, He says, *A new command I give you: Love one another. As I have loved you, so you must love one another (John 13:34-35).* Here I was again, back to being confronted by it is either the fear of man, or the fear of God. The goal of studying Scripture is not knowledge for knowledge's sake, it's to ultimately know how to love people. Loving people is a prerequisite to loving God, 1 John 4:20-21:

> *Whoever claims to love God yet hates a brother or sister is a
> liar. For whoever does not love their brother and sister,
> whom they have seen, cannot love God, whom they have not
> seen. And he has given us this command: Anyone who loves
> God must also love their brother and sister.*

This lesson has been unfolding in my life too. As I have been learning, loving people sometimes goes against cultural expectations or norms. Peter the head of the early church, also struggled with this, choosing to fear men and please them over loving like God commanded, pleasing God. As stated in Galatians 2:12-13, *he (Peter) began to draw back and separate himself from the Gentiles because he was afraid of those who belonged to the circumcision group. The other Jews joined him in his hypocrisy.*

Loving Heart or Pleasing Man

God then led me to Luke 10:27-28, where an expert in the Jewish law said that the greatest command is to love God and love your neighbor. Jesus replied:

You have answered correctly. Do this and you will **live.**
Luke 10:28

This hit me profoundly. I felt truly alive — I live — so I felt I was loving as God desires me to do. I feel this full life I am living and blessed with is directly tied to God opening my heart to love people. It takes courage to love, I had found that out! For me, it was the most bold and courageous thing I could do, loving others, and God knew that — so He had challenged me in that specific area. I encourage you to pray and ask God to fill your heart with radical love for others, if you have the courage. Yes, that is a challenge, it truly does take courage. As you love, your life will change, and you will come alive as Jesus promised. I want you to truly live — fully and abundantly, this best life ever. Loving others, has been the greatest blessing in my life. As this occurs and I know people closer and care more, my intimacy with God grows exponentially as I am loving what God, and now I, together love — all people. We share this common bond of love and care for people, pulling me closer to God's side. It tightly binds my heart to the heart of God, allowing me to walk closely at His side on this great path.

When you walk with God, you will love like God.

Now this may shock you, it did me, as I processed through this. The opposite is also true. If I do not love people, like God, I am not walking with God. Let that sink in, as it is a simple test to see if we are walking with Him, or not. This challenged me, as obviously I do not walk with Him every minute of the day. I choose not to love, at times frustrated by the people around me. In those moments I step off the path, away from His presence, no longer at His side. God patiently waits for me to return, and at times like a good father He will discipline me. May God open our eyes to this reality.

What is Maturity in Christ? LOVE

God continued to focus my heart on love, bringing me back to 1 Corinthians 13. I kept reading it over and over, letting it sink in how essential love is. Paul, a man, wrote this glorious passage on love—I believe, the most beautiful words about love ever written. Paul is 100% a man's man. Tough, hard, strong, blunt, adventurer, survivor, brilliant theologian, and yet overflowing with tender compassionate love for all people. *He was mature.* May we be mature loving like Paul. In 1 Corinthians 13, Paul makes it clear, nothing else—whether it's having all knowledge and truth, doing miraculous works, or speaking impressive sermons or speeches—compares to having love. Verse 11 hit home for me, was I a mature follower of God, or still a child?

> *When I was a child, I talked like a child,*
> *I thought like a child, I reasoned like a child.*
> *When I became a man, I put childish ways behind me.*
> *1 Corinthians 13:11*

Maturity is described as understanding how love is greater than everything else. I felt like God was shaping me into a man, finally maturing, in this new understanding of love. Here is a funny story related to love and maturity—about 30 years ago when we first got married. Annually I focused on to master just one attribute of love from 1 Corinthians 13, then move on to the next. The list of attributes is: love is patient, love is kind, and so on. Well, it's been 30 years and I still haven't gotten past the first one, to be more patient! Loving is hard work. I'm realizing that maturity isn't about knowledge or grand actions—it's about loving others. Look at your life, how mature are you in your faith, your love? The standard is compassionate love for others.

Paul echoes this again in Galatians when he criticizes religious leaders for caring more about tradition than loving others. Paul was beyond frustrated at these leaders, preferring they be castrated if they continued to walk without love! He then summarizes and writes:

> *Serve one another humbly in love.*
> *For the entire law is fulfilled in keeping this one command:*
> *'Love your neighbor as yourself.'*
> *Galatians 5:13-14*

The entire law, *ALL* of God's commandments, is summed up in just two words:

Love Others
That's it. Let us not overcomplicate it!

God then brought me to 1 John 4:8, which reminds us that *God is love.* I started to put these puzzle pieces together. If I follow God, walking at His side, and He is described as love, the fruit of that will naturally be me loving others. This reminded me what our youngest son told us when he was in high school,

show me your friends, and I will show you your future

Who we walk by, we become. As we walk with God, we become like God, full of love. If we are not full of this love, well, obviously we are not walking closely with God. My maturity, my likeness to God — is measured by how well I love people.

The Puzzle takes Shape

The lens through which I view the world became clearer, as I realized God's constant mandate to love. In writing this, I remember what a friend in Poland earlier in March had seen as she prayed for me,

I see you getting on lots of flights, much travel, assembling a large puzzle, slowly collecting the pieces. Then suddenly the puzzle comes together and you can see the full picture.

As with any large puzzle, you start on the outside, the border pieces, then work toward the middle. I feel the outline of this puzzle is slowly taking shape.

The borders are most definitely in the shape of a heart.

It is the outline of God, love! God gives us a choice, to have His loving heart, or to conform to the world. What is your choice? Have courage, as following and giving the love of God is the key that will give you the best life ever. It also empowers you to have a life of purpose, transforming the world.

The outline of God is a HEART... Love!

Chapter 38

Do Not Miss the Call
(Day 25)

*The Lord said to Moses, send some men to explore the
land of Canaan, which I am giving to the Israelites...*

*But the men who had gone up with him said, we can't
attack those people. They are stronger than we are...*

*As surely as I live declares the Lord...
Not one of you will enter the land....
In this desert your bodies will fall...*

EXCERPTS FROM NUMBERS 13 AND 14

Sunday's sermon moved me. It was about the nation of Israel, who were given a promise and a calling by God. They came to the border of the promised land, ready to claim that promise, but when they saw the challenges ahead, *fear overtook them, and they refused to follow in obedience.* As a result, God took the promise away. They never saw the glorious promise fulfilled, instead they lived the rest of their days in the horribly dry desert and died there. I know what a desert is, as we live in Phoenix, Arizona, in the USA. Summer temperatures can be up to 120F/49C. I will not live spiritually in the desert and die there due to refusing to follow. God is faithful to His promises, but we also need to be faithful to obey. In 1 Corinthians 10:5 it talks about how Israel did not obey God saying: *God was not pleased with **most** of them; their bodies were scattered over the desert.* The word, *most*, hit me. The majority of the believers in the nation of

Israel did not follow or obey God, and the result was that their dead bodies were scattered over the desert. That graphically paints a horrible picture that should put the healthy fear of God in us. We should not look to see where the crowd of believers is going, or we also could join them dying in the desert. God may not leave the door open forever for you to follow Him, or to receive what He promised, if you do not obey.

There is a cost to follow.
*…but, a much higher cost to **not** follow.*

I reflected on my own life and the promises God had made to me. I realized that I too, needed to obey Him and step forward into what He had called me to do. Yet, I was facing a personal challenge again; it was fear of man. My calling, this path, feels very mysterious and unusual, not what I see others around me called to. I feel odd, awkward, even as I see miracle after miracle unfold. The question on my heart was whether I would press forward in faith and continue following God, or let fear hold me back. These thoughts swirled in my mind as we went to lunch with another couple after the church service.

Unexpected Talk

At lunch, while sitting with the couple, their children, and my wife, I went to refill my water. As I walked past our waitress, Julia, God highlighted her to me. Without much thought, I asked her a simple question, *How long have you worked here?* Her eyes lit up as she began sharing about her time at the restaurant and her other job. She even gave recommendations for live music venues in the area. We had a short talk, and I felt prompted to tell her about the church service we had just attended. I also mentioned an upcoming event at the church for young people about her age.

She was intrigued, explaining that she had never been to church before and wondered if there were any requirements to attend. I smiled and told her, *as long as you have a heartbeat, you qualify.* Her face brightened, as it was clear she longed for community and friendships with people her age. She looked at the website and said she would think about going.

Be Prepared: Not all will Express Excitement at the Miracle

When I returned to the table, I briefly summarized what had just happened, expecting the others to share in my excitement. To my surprise, they simply said, *That's great* and went back to their conversation, seemingly unmoved by the encounter. I felt I had seen a miracle occur, heaven break through the clouds and touch the earth. God opening a heart of a young lady He dearly loves, and He had used me to speak His words to her. It was glorious! I felt like my face was glowing, just as Moses' had after encountering God on Mount Sinai. So, *That's great* was not what I hoped they would say. They had not seen or felt the miracle themselves, so to them it was just a story. We have to be prepared for this and realize this is usually what happens. I continue to struggle with this, expecting (wrongly!) that all will be filled with the same level of amazement at what God had done. It is not appropriate for me to expect this, as they were not there seeing God work. So, I quietly returned to my meal, still amazed at what had just occurred, grateful for the moment, even if I was the only one who saw it.

To see God. To hear God. To know God. To follow God. We must keep our eyes attentive to watch how God is working around us, or we will miss His call, His promises, and the glory that comes with it. Do not fear, just follow.

Prime Minister Winston Churchill of the United Kingdom famously said during World War II,
The only thing we have to fear, is fear itself.

Move forward toward your call.
You want the promise; you do not want the scorching desert!

Have fear, great fear — of fear!

Chapter 39

Joy in Pain
(Day 26 - 27)

Let us fix our eyes on Jesus…
who for the joy set before him endured the cross
HEBREWS 12:2

What a day it was! A series of four back-to-back, remarkable meetings. First, meeting with the recently retired lead political lobbyist from Intel Corporation. Then, speaking with a former Deputy National Security Advisor for the US President, then a retired senior official from the US State Department, and finally, a senior lawyer and tax expert who works with wealthy donors. I couldn't believe I had the chance to do video calls with these amazing people. In each meeting, I had the privilege of praying for them, and they felt blessed, as I did. It was truly incredible—a day filled with rich blessings.

Over the summer, I also had the honor of spending time with dear friends, Bob and Karen, both in their 80s. Decades ago, they had blessed us as they led the Newly Married Class at our church, and now it was our turn to bless them. Bob and Karen were missionaries in Brazil and later became school teachers before retiring more than a decade ago. They now face significant health challenges, and I had the privilege of accompanying them to various doctor's appointments. The treasure though was, being their spiritual son and praying for them—and they for me. It feels like stepping into heaven when we are in their presence.

Even in Pain, with God we can Rest

Bob and Karen often feel their lives have lost value due to age and physical limitations. Sitting beside them, gently holding Karen's hand as she rests on the couch next to her loving husband, I had the opportunity to tenderly remind her of God's incredible love. This week, God gave me the words to tell her that He sees her as His beautiful daughter, a princess of the King. She doesn't need to do anything to earn His love—her presence alone brings Him such great joy. I spoke of how God treasures her, how her husband Bob's constant care is a reflection of Jesus' love for her, and how her husband loves her. Tears filled both of our eyes as I finished, and Karen smiled, saying, *The pain is gone! I shall not fear; I am a daughter of the King. Jesus loves me.* Bob who was sitting next to her, tenderly kissed her hand. It was like sitting beside a fragrant flower, Karen a royal princess. Bob, always by her side, held her other hand and told her how much he loved her.

Karen later shared a moving story with me. One night, as she lay in bed with pain coursing through her body—a condition she endures most of the time—she cried out to God for relief. As soon as her head hit the pillow, the pain vanished, and she slept. In her dream, the pain returned, but as she prayed, it disappeared again. When she awoke the next morning, the pain was back, and she asked God why He had allowed it to return. She felt Him gently tell her that He wanted to show her that He has power over the pain and could take it away, but had chosen to let it remain. Even though the pain persisted, knowing that God was in control gave her peace. She felt loved by God, even in the midst of suffering.

Knowing God is in control gives us rest

This profound story resonates with most of us who experience pain, whether for a season or a lifetime. Like Karen, we want the pain to go away. I want my emotional and relational pain to be gone. I wish it would just leave and I have prayed for it to. Yet, God has gently told me it may never leave and that is His will, as the pain will keep me humble, weak, and dependent on Him. This has confused me. As I write this I can think of two areas of pain, that arrived in force this year. No one longs for unnecessary pain. The pain though holds a hidden blessing, it is a necessity, as it is used by God to mature us and complete us, but we have to be honest, pain hurts! These trials, this pain, may never leave. Let me repeat, the pain of your life may never leave. Is God enough for us, even in the continual pain? As we mature, His love slowly fills us as we become like Him. The joy of walking with Him displaces the pain, as His love fills us. I am slowly understanding the *pure joy* talked about in this challenging passage in James 1:2-4, and slowly my attitude is changing. Embracing the trials and pain willingly (honestly though, I am not quite with *pure joy* yet!), knowing that on the other side great blessing awaits.

Consider it pure joy, my brothers and sisters,
whenever you face trials of many kinds, because you know
that the testing of your faith produces perseverance.
Let perseverance finish its work so that you may be
mature and complete, not lacking anything.

I wish there was a way to be mature and complete without pain, *there is not*. There will be suffering, as God transforms you into his masterpiece. All world-class Olympic athletes know this: pain is required to achieve the prize. Go forward; the prize is worth it! God has called and designed you to be a world-class follower, His strong athlete, to be on the field of life experiencing a full life. The pain is just rocks on the path. Run for the prize! The great news is, this prize, the joy of walking with God, starts here right now on earth. In heaven it will only get better.

Run!

Run in such a way as to get the prize.
1 Corinthians 9:24

Chapter 40

Following Alone
(Day 28-29)

I did not immediately consult with anyone...
Then after three years I went up to Jerusalem
GALATIANS 1:16,18

Paul the Apostle had a radical experience. When he came to know Jesus, he was blinded and Jesus appeared to him. In a few days he miraculously regained his sight and then immediately went alone to a foreign land. I'm sure those around him thought he was crazy for going alone. I could relate.

On the couch, my thoughts kept circling around the sermon about Israel losing the promise, my calling, and the fear of moving forward with what God had asked me to do. My wife loves me deeply, and I shared with her the callings I believe are from God for my life. They are not typical, father, husband, family man sort of things. All this was very unsettling for her. She was worried that if I continued down this path, there might be pain. I am blessed beyond measure to have a wife who is nurturing, loving, and wholly dedicated to caring for me and our two boys. Her life's calling is to love us and ensure we're well taken care of. So, when I decided to follow God's call - a path that she felt was risky, and is out of the ordinary, she understandably wasn't excited.

After a long and emotional conversation, my wife — through tears — spoke these words to me:

You go for it... I will just pray... Feel free to pursue it...

As all this unfolded, God reminded me of a question He had asked me almost a year earlier in December 2023. I was in a meeting when I suddenly felt God asking, *would you leave your family behind to follow Me?* That question made me feel immediately sick, nauseated. My family is my top priority, period. I love my wife and boys, and my life revolves around them to nurture, protect and to lift them up. I asked God for confirmation if I had heard that question correctly. He delivered it hours later through a friend, who shared a vision they had had while praying, hearing, *Your friend Craig hasn't been asked to choose between following Me or his family yet, but he soon will.* That was incredibly difficult to hear, but was the confirmation I needed. Over the next two days, I spent hours talking to God in prayer. I asked Him if there was a different way, but I felt Him just repeating the words, *come – follow me.*

Before the weekend was over, I made the difficult decision to follow God. Even as it meant offering up what I hold dearest, precious time with family and their full understanding of my calling. Earlier in the year, February 2023, I had made a vow to God in Rome stating:

Lord, I will go where you want me to go.
Lord, I will do what you want me to do.

God now was calling me on this vow, and I knew it. It was painfully hard. It forced me to realize I had placed spending time with my family above loving and obeying God. God knew that and was calling me to change that, desiring I place Him first in my heart. This was extremely difficult for me, crushing me. The first of the Ten Commandments clearly says, *You shall have no other gods before Me. (Exodus 20:3)* Loving your family is commanded by God, but loving them more than loving and obeying God is where things go wrong. Following means dying to our will, and God knew exactly what needed to die. That weekend in December 2023, I made a covenant with God, that I would follow His call, even if it meant leaving my family behind, not even fully realizing what all that meant. I would find out in 2024, multiple times. It was one of the hardest decisions I've ever made, but God reminded me of His words as

I reflected on this: *The Lord will fight for you; you need only to be still (Exodus 14:14).* Being fully transparent, this is all still very hard for me, it is painful, very hard to write this. It helped me to better understand the verses in 1 Corinthians 7:29,35 where Paul is telling all people, married or single, to seek God's will first.

> *From now on those who have wives*
> *should live as if they had none…*
> *that you may live in a right way*
> *in undivided devotion to the Lord*

Rejoicing in the Middle of the Mystery

As I was praying there on the couch, after the difficult emotional talk with my wife, I felt God then told me very specifically to obey Him and *rejoice*. What?!?! He commanded me not to pray that my wife or that others would agree with me, but to rejoice as He will take care of this situation. I must rejoice, He said, and focus on following Him. This was incredibly difficult, and I now was completely drained. He had made the path straight and clear, but I sure didn't like it

> *Trust in the Lord with all your heart, and lean not on your*
> *own understanding; in all your ways acknowledge him and*
> *he will make your path straight.*
> PROVERBS 3:5-6

I was determined though to walk the path, even if in fear. Proverbs 1:7 says, *The fear of the Lord is the beginning of wisdom* and that's how I moved forward — much more in fear than in joy at that moment.

God also reminded me of Jesus' words in the Gospel of John: *You must follow Me (John 21:22).* There was no alternative, I **MUST** follow Him. It was not a request, it was an order from God, and I would not disobey God. I was learning what the *fear of the Lord* is, it is obedience even when we do not want to obey. Despite the lack of joy, I had to keep following and try to somehow rejoice.

That evening, feeling overwhelmed, I cried out to God, *HELP, Lord! What can I do?*, I wrote in my journal. God's response was immediate: *Wait, and rejoice.* What?!?!, I thought, again God says this? I thought to myself, *wait, rejoice, that feels like I am doing nothing.* That is not easy, to rejoice when a heart is grieving and God doesn't even want me to pray. On the couch right then, I committed to writing a list of 10 things I was grateful for. I started writing, and 51 items later, my hand was tired, but my heart was full of joy, I wrote in my journal, *Haha! How, Lord, you revive a hurting heart!*

A verse came to mind: *Then Jesus declared, 'I am the bread of life. Whoever comes to Me will never go hungry, and whoever believes in Me will never be thirsty' (John 6:35).* In that moment of writing 51 praises, I felt spiritually fed and satisfied, as I had come to Him. In this pain, I was becoming one with God, participating not just in His blessings but also in sufferings, just like Jesus did. By feeding on His word, His voice, and His life, I felt joy rush into my heart, even though my circumstances and the storm around me, hadn't changed at all. I wrote, *Lord, as I feed on You, Your Word, Your voice, Your life fills me. None of my circumstances have changed, but feeding on You gives me such joy. 'The Spirit gives life' (John 6:63) is so true!*

None of this was a random accident. I would soon realize there was a reason. God was reminding me of my calling and the vow I made to follow Him despite obstacles. I had reaffirmed that vow to follow on this day. It was all in preparation, as just days later, He suddenly would call me to go to Washington D.C. to pray, even though I had just returned from a trip to Asia. Every step of the way, God was showing me that this journey, no matter how challenging and mysterious, was completely orchestrated and planned by Him, and He would walk with me on it.

I must follow Him, even if alone.

Therefore, my dear brothers and sisters, stand firm.
Let nothing move you.
Always give yourselves fully to the work of the Lord,
because you know that your labor in the Lord is not in vain.
1 CORINTHIANS 15:58

Chapter 41

God Calls the One
(Day 30)

I have called you by name, you are mine.
ISAIAH 43:1

Friday morning and I was excited. I had a video call scheduled with Saachi; someone I hadn't spoken to in months. It was truly a miracle how God had connected us over a year ago. She is a knowledgeable Diversity Manager at a large California company and had reached out for help in getting her company to approve faith and religion-based employee resource groups. Given my experience speaking at conferences on this topic, she had found my name and contact information. We had a great first meeting. Saachi grew up as a Hindu but said she now feels more like an agnostic. She had Christian friends at her workplace and she'd attended a few Bible studies, fascinated by the way Christians behave.

At the end of our first meeting about a year ago, I asked if I could pray for her. She hesitated, then agreed. Over the video call I prayed, and by the end of it her eyes had tears forming, as she said how beautiful it was and how she could feel the love. It was such a powerful moment I am sure she will always remember, as I will. Likely that was a new experience, never having anyone pray for her like that.

Fast-forward to today—I was eager to catch up with her again. We shared updates on our lives, including my recent trip to Asia and her upcoming trip to Asia. She told me about her work situation, how her management had rejected the idea of a religious or faith-based employee group, even though they allowed other groups like a women's group and an LGBTQ+ group. Companies are often not aware, or choose to ignore that faith and religion are an important part of over 80% of all Americans, and even higher globally. We also talked about God a little, and, just like last time, at the end I asked if I could pray for her. She agreed, and I prayed, blessing her in prayer. At the *Amen!* a huge smile covered her face, and I think an even bigger smile was on mine. It was such an enjoyable time talking. We decided to reconnect in a few months and continue our conversation. She told me how much she enjoyed talking with me, and how much life she felt in our discussions.

Amen. God truly works in incredible ways. The amazing part is that as I was writing this chapter, I received a text message from Saachi, a video of her eating a meal of flaming ramen noodles in Japan as she is vacationing there. When we love like Christ, it builds relationships and opens doors in the most unexpected and wonderful ways. The flames from that noodle dish were huge!

God loves Saachi and is calling her by name, may we also treat others in this personal way like God does, **one on one.**

Chapter 42

Diving In
(Day 31)

My heart is racing and my knees are weak
as I walk to the edge,
I know there is no turning back
once my feet have left the ledge,
In the rush I hear a voice that's telling me
it's time to take the leap of faith.
So here I go, I'm diving in,
I'm going deep,
in over my head I wanna be
Caught in the rush
lost in the flow,
in over my head I wanna go.
The river's deep, the river's wide,
the river's water is alive,
So sink or swim,
I'm diving in

"DIVE" BY STEVEN CURTIS CHAPMAN

Again, I sat on the couch early in the morning. You will notice that I usually sit in the same spot (my couch) during the same time of the day (morning). This helps me quickly connect to God. My body knows that this is where I daily sit in His presence. In churchy words this is called a place of abiding or communing with God. It is important to be consistent, as it helps you make these precious moments with God count.

For some reason I had this song *Dive* playing, it was my fourth time listening to it. It was written decades ago, and I'm not sure even how or why I played it that morning, but it touched me. The music was turned up loud on the stereo, with the surround sound and two subwoofers working well, the world around me faded. I could only hear God's voice, clear and unwavering, telling me to dive in. He wanted me in Washington D.C. to pray. It was the morning of Saturday, October 19, 2024, and He was calling me to leave in just four days. I felt Him giving me clear instructions; I was to take a Wednesday night flight, arrive Thursday morning, and leave Sunday night. God was asking me to just follow, yet I hesitated, like a child standing at the edge, looking down at the flowing water below.

Tears streamed down my face as I sat there, eyes closed, listening to God and the song. I felt that He was sitting there next to me on the couch. I finally said *yes* to God, I would dive into that river to follow. At that exact moment my wife gently tapped me on the shoulder to comfort me, as she saw me weeping on the couch. I jumped, startled, my arms and legs flailing in all directions. My decision scared her, and it scared me too. I knew though I had to follow, I had heard His call to jump, and I would not get out of the river.

Reese Howell – The Praying Intercessor

God knows where we are weak and how to support us. The day before, I had been unexpectedly invited to a conference in the Phoenix area. I attended, enjoying a steak dinner under the stars at a beautiful resort while listening to a professional singer sing hymns. At dinner, I sat next to a man named Jon. We didn't seem to have much in common, but as I shared how God had called me to travel and pray for people and nations in places like Italy, Israel, Poland, Korea, and China, Jon suddenly said, *Craig, have you ever heard of the book Reese Howell Intercessor? It sounds like God is calling you in the same way.* What surprised me was that Jon was the third person to mention this book to me in the last month. I had read it over 40 years ago as a teenager, and had not thought or heard of it for that length of time. Now I felt it was clear, God wanted me to read it again. I began to read the book, and much of it felt like my life! It became evident that it was about a man who was called by God to do amazing, but unusual things, especially related to prayer, and great things happened because of it. Reese Howell lived in the United Kingdom during World War II, and the prayers he and his group prayed changed the world. It sounded strikingly like my own calling: to pray and follow God.

In the book, over a century ago, Reese heard God calling him to just follow with all of his life:

Remember Reese, your will must go.
On no account will I allow you to bring in a crosscurrent.
Where I send you, you will go;
what I say to you, you will do.

Vow to God

In February 2023, in Rome, I had made a vow to the Lord, almost identical in wording, as I knelt on the cobblestones of St. Peter's Square on a cold Sunday night:

Lord, I will go where you want me to go.
Lord, I will do what you want me to do.

Immediately after saying these words, this vow to God, the bells tolled 8 times, beautifully echoing within the cold empty plaza in front of St Peter's Basilica. It was surreal. I would later learn that the number 8 was significant, signifying the start of a new life. A new life of radical following had begun there in Rome, with the latest command being to go to Washington D.C.

I must go. The words from Mark Batterson's *Draw the Circle: The 40 Day Prayer Challenge* flooded my mind, words that had changed my life. These words were originally told to a young man named D.L. Moody born in 1837, propelling him to tell over 100 million globally in his preaching about the love of Jesus.

The world has yet to see what God will do
with and for and through and in and by
the man who is fully and wholly consecrated to Him.

I had asked for God to make me that man. He had heard me. Now He was doing it. I guess I should not have been surprised.

Prayer: God's Words not Mine

That evening, as usual, my wife and I read a verse from the Bible and prayed for each other. I shared how I felt odd praying for so many people and nations, caring for all so much, as my prayers were just average. My wife, with her few but powerful words, said, *Do not doubt! It is God who speaks through you, not you.* I was moved. Thank you, Lord, for my wife.

As I pondered her words, I remembered two Bible verses she had perfectly summarized:

But God chose the foolish things of the world to shame the wise; God chose the weak things of the world to shame the strong.
1 CORINTHIANS 1:27

In the same way, the Spirit helps us in our weakness. We do not know what we ought to pray for, but the Spirit himself intercedes for us with groans that words cannot express. And he who searches our hearts knows the mind of the Spirit, because the Spirit intercedes for the saints in accordance with God's will.
ROMANS 8:26-27

That is how I felt at times; foolish, weak, unsure what to pray for or say. God takes our simple words and prayers, and through the Holy Spirit they are transformed, penetrating into hearts, lives, and even nations — changing world events. Do not doubt! It isn't your words, you are the pipe, the path, the conduit God uses for His amazing loving powerful words to flow. God spoke, and the universe was formed. His words are *power*, and they will flow through you as you partner with God! It is a mystery — like how we see the impact of the wind, but we do not understand where it came from or where it is going. That night, despite the chaos around me, I went to sleep with peace in my heart.

I had dove into the water.

I was wet in the river of His will, and flowing with Him.

Chapter 43

Investment Ratio 1 to 100 (Day 32)

He heals the brokenhearted and binds up their wounds.
PSALM 147:3

As His followers, we are being transformed into the likeness of Jesus. As such, we are called to heal the brokenhearted. The process is simple: we *see, listen, love*. God does the rest. It is a partnership with God, we open the door and He pours through.

For the past year, I've been attending a small church that places a strong emphasis on relationships and prayer. On Sundays, I'm filled with excitement to go. Each time, I find myself engaged in listening and praying for people, and this Sunday was no exception. God often highlights individuals to me, and our conversations almost always end in prayer.

The day began with a friend, who shared the answer to a prayer we had prayed about a month ago regarding her job. I was overjoyed to hear that she had received a new job with a 25% higher salary than she had expected. During the service in a time of prayer, I felt I should go forward to pray for another friend, who had come to the front for prayer along with others. God had highlighted her to me, so I prayed for her, and she received the prayer with tears, feeling lifted and encouraged.

Newly Engaged!

The church service is over 2 hours long, so there's a break in the middle for coffee. During this break, I found myself talking with Abby in the hallway. God had highlighted her as someone

I should talk to, and the timing was perfect. Abby, early 40s, had just been proposed to the day before, and she was getting married soon. She began to share her incredible journey, including a liver transplant two years ago when she was close to death. Recently she had been on a trip to Africa, where she learned that financial poverty is just one of five areas of impoverishment. In Africa, she had met people without food, yet filled with joy and close relationships, beyond rich, but hungry. We talked about her trip and her unexpected exciting move toward marriage, and I could see the radiant joy on her face. I asked if I could pray for her, as I looked at her ring she had just received the day prior, I prayed for her marriage and life. We smiled and returned to the service as it was nearing its end.

Healing Presence and Healing Touch

Another miraculous moment happened when I saw Chloe again. Two months earlier, God had highlighted her to me at church when it was her first time there, and I had prayed for her. Her story is remarkable: she had stopped at the church during a 12-hour drive between Arizona and another state. What!?!? No one does that, but Chloe did. As we stood in the hallway that Sunday, I prayed for her. At first, I wasn't sure what God wanted me to say and I was awkwardly silent. Chloe responded, *you don't have to say a thing, just be here.* She then asked me to pray by placing my hand on her forehead. As I prayed, God gave me His words, and she began to smile and laugh, fully being filled with God's joy. Most of the time I was silent as she stood there with eyes closed in the hall, radiating the joy of Jesus.

We had just finished praying in the hallway, when we met Gary, who rolled up in his wheelchair. Chloe and I knelt beside him on the concrete there in the hall, then moved to chairs as the prayer time extended. We listened to his difficult journey. Gary had felt unsafe his entire life, enduring physical and emotional abuse from both men and women. As we spoke and prayed, I felt led to place my hand on his shoulder and I held His hand. Chloe did the same on the other side. As we continued, Gary suddenly looked up and said, *You have no idea what's going on here!* When I asked him to explain, he shared how in the past, when someone touched him, he would jump and feel nervous due to all the physical abuse. Yet, with us, he felt peace for the first time in his life. His eyes filled with tears. He had not realized it prior, but he had been craving human connection, including touch. A little later, he burst out saying, *I truly think I'm healed. I feel safe being touched!* We continued to pray, and I felt led to ask him, *why did God choose you and protect you all these years? Why Gary?* At first, Gary responded with reasons like *to help others*, or *I can do many things*. God kept telling me to keep repeating the question to him, and as I continued to repeat the same question, he broke down in tears. Finally exclaiming, *it is because God loves me!* Gary is a strong man, and he hammered his head into my chest, burying it as he wept. It was a powerful moment, and both Chloe and I began to weep with him.

As I left to get tissues in the bathroom, as we truly all needed them, God impressed on my heart that I had to pray for Gary's physical healing, to get out of the wheelchair. Earlier in the church service that day, I had felt led to pray for him to be healed, but I had not moved as praying like that scared me. Now I knew God was ordering me to pray. I looked at myself in the mirror, with a huge wad of tissues in my hand, and I looked quite nervous. Yet, I told the Lord whatever He wanted me to do, I will do. When I returned, I asked Gary if we could continue praying. To my surprise, he said, *I'm overwhelmed. I want to stop now. I'm hungry and need to process all of this.* After Gary had left, Chloe mentioned that she also had heard God telling her that we were to pray for his physical healing, exactly what I had heard. It was amazing and often like the stories in the Bible, where God prioritized healing a heart, teaching Gary how to receive love, before healing his physical body. Two weeks later, Gary approached me in his wheelchair, saying, *I feel completely safe now, and I know where I feel safe.* When I asked him where that was, he said, *right here at church, because I feel like Jesus' arms are wrapped around me. In His arms, I feel safe.* Amen!

Fully Surrender, and God's Response – a Kiss

I then had time to pray with Chloe. In that moment, I felt led to surrender again every part of my life again to God. He wanted me to, and I complied. With hands cupped forward as if giving, I slowly prayed and gave everything to Him—my family, money, health, dreams, pleasure, honor, and desires, everything of value I could think of. When I felt I had given it all to God, I asked God to help me receive all of His blessings, as I struggled with receiving. Immediately after praying this, to my amazement, Chloe began to laugh. It was hard for her to talk as she was laughing so much. She slowly explained that as I prayed with my hands open, giving item by item to God, she saw Him receive it, kiss it, then give it back to me placing it in my open hands. She said God had told her not to mention this to me, but when I asked God to teach me how to receive, then she was set free to tell me.

Tears filled my eyes as I marveled at God's faithfulness. It felt like a test, like the one given to Abraham when God asked him to sacrifice his son. Abraham was willing, and so was I, to give up what I most treasured to follow His calling. God's response to Abraham was,

> *Now I know that you fear God,*
> *because you have not withheld from me your son,*
> *your only son*
> GENESIS 22:12

Fearing God is something I always struggled with understanding. Fearing God is about obeying Him, even when it's difficult. Especially as you follow Christ more, He will ask you to do things you absolutely do not want to do. Get ready, it takes courage. For me, it meant surrendering time with my family. Then just to make sure He had all of me, everything else I held dear I needed to offer to Him. I passed the test, in tears. I couldn't help but wonder if Chloe, who I really didn't know much, was an angel of some sort. She had suddenly appeared, and just as suddenly had left, to continue driving that day for another 9 hours. Yet, we had worked together in prayer and blessed Gary as if we had known each other for years, all through our common partnership with God.

The interconnectedness of the body of Christ never ceases to amaze me. Following God opens this door, and it is a door leading to a life full of His joy, walking in His presence, with dear brothers and sister! Is there pain, yes, but oh the joy! Reflecting on all that had happened, I felt incredibly blessed and in awe of how God had worked.

As I had obeyed and prayed for others, I received a hundredfold in return. I had been a Corporate Finance Controller and a Strategic Finance Analyst, **a return of 100x on any investment is always good!**

Chapter 44

Delighting in Fear

he will delight in the fear of the Lord
ISAIAH 11:3

No one wants more fear… or do they?

It was a bright sunny day, but John didn't notice, he was in college and until a few minutes ago having a great day. He was distracted as he quickly walked across the parking lot, dodging through parked cars, replying to a text from his irate girlfriend. He had forgotten that her birthday was yesterday, and she was letting him know in no uncertain terms. John knew he better text back quickly before she sent another scathing text. Walking fast through the parked cars, he tried to type quickly, swearing in frustration at the autocorrect as it was selecting the wrong words. He quickly stepped out from behind the large truck and didn't see the car flying through the parking lot going way too fast; the horn blared…

Having Fear can be a Gift

Fear can save us from threats that could harm us, and it can open the door to blessing. Sometimes we fear things we should not, that is not good, but the fear described in the Bible is a very good thing, *you want lots of fear of God!* Yes! The more fear of God the better! Bring it on!

Does being excited to have fear confuse you? It confused me, up until these last two years. It is very important to talk about this, as you have seen during this journey where many times I have absolutely not wanted to follow God's call. Yet I obeyed and followed due to fear of God. I never want to hear God say to me, *You failed to follow and obey Me.* That I do fear! Just following has a healthy dose of fearing God in it, you need this.

I have read about *the fear of the Lord* many times in the Bible. The passages talk about how it is such a great thing, bringing wisdom and so many other benefits. In these two years of travel and God commanding me to do things I would not have chosen to do; I feel I am finally understanding.

On January 9, 2019 — Vimbai, a friend at work who grew up in Zimbabwe, and who leads the Intel Christian groups in Arizona prayed this over me. *Side Note – how do I know the exact date? I write in my Bible a lot; remembering God's promises are key, I recommend you do the same!*

He prayed this, Isaiah 11:2
> *The spirit of the Lord will rest on him,*
> *the spirit of wisdom and of understanding,*
> *the spirit of counsel and of power,*
> *the spirit of knowledge and the fear of the Lord.*

Powerful verse, I liked it, saying loudly *Amen!*

My friend continued, reading the next verse, Isaiah 11:3:
> *and he will **delight in the fear of the Lord**.*

I did not say *Amen* after that.

Surprisingly, in this Bible passage there was not a lot of delighting in wisdom, understanding, counsel and power. That is what I would have been most happy to receive. What you delight in, is your treasure. What is this delight in fearing God?

Fearing God is Obeying God

Following is obeying God, so you need this fear of God also. The fear part comes in frequently. Often, we do not want to obey God. You will want to obey God, even in fear, for these reasons.

- Avoid Pain - *think of a car racing toward you*
- Receive a blessing - *His blessings are good!*
- Closer to Him – *it is a test, with a blessing, His presence!*

Do not be fooled; the longer you follow God, *the more fearful things He will ask you to do*. In courage though you will move forward, as you know ultimately it will be good.

Fearing God: Helps us Avoid Pain

Imagine a speeding car coming toward you—fear is what keeps you safe. Similarly, fearing God protects us from pain. The Bible teaches that those who have received the knowledge of God but continue to disobey His commands will face severe consequences. You do not want to experience that!

> *If we deliberately keep on sinning after we have received the knowledge of the truth, no sacrifice for sins is left, but only a fearful expectation of judgment and of raging fire that will consume the enemies of God.*
> HEBREWS 10:26-27

This strong language is meant to instill in us a healthy fear, motivating us to obey Him and avoid pain. Consider the Ten Commandments, which instruct us not to lie, commit adultery, covet, or engage in other behaviors God forbids. Ignoring these commandments is like stepping in front of a speeding car—you will get hurt. Fearing and obeying God spares us from much suffering both in this life and for eternity.

Fearing God: Helps us Receive a Blessing

Fearing God and stepping out in faith, even when it means doing something you don't want to do, is a powerful act of obedience. Following reveals that we love and trust God. As James 2:17 reminds us, *faith by itself, if it does not result in action, is dead.* When we move forward in obedient faith—despite our fear—it shows Him our love.

> *Jesus replied, "All who love me will do what I say. My Father will love them, and we will come and make our home with each of them."*
> JOHN 14: 23

Obedience is significant to God! We want God's love and for Him to come and make His home with us. He loves us as His children, and often, He pours out blessings from heaven when we obey, even if we do so with fear. Although blessings here on earth are not guaranteed every time we step out in fearful obedience, many times God does honor our faith with His favor. Test Him, and you'll see! Proverbs 22:4 states: *Humility and fearing the Lord, bring wealth and honor and life.*

A personal example is when 30 years ago God clearly called me to live in Brazil for a year. I had a little fear, but my parents, especially my mother was terrified. She feared the worst, imagining I'd be eaten by piranhas! To go there, I had to sell my car, use all my savings, close a retirement account (paying a penalty), leave my close friends, move to a country that was at times dangerous, live where I didn't speak the language, and I didn't know where I would even stay. Any reasonable person would have been afraid! However, I was excited as I had heard God clearly say to go. God didn't tell me there would be a great blessing, I just followed. The incredible blessing would be that I would date and marry my pen-pal, gaining the most amazing wife! What if I had not obeyed? I believe I would have missed the glorious blessing of marrying my Brazilian wife. We never know what blessings He has in store for us on the other side of the pain and fear.

It's like being asked to cross over on one of two equally scary, old rope bridges hanging over a terrifying dark canyon. You feel pretty sure God is asking you to take the bridge on the right, but you are not 100% certain. Still, you begin walking across that bridge, not knowing whether it's to avoid pain, receive a blessing, or simply be tested in your faith. Yet you go forward, trusting and obeying.

Remember, courage is not the absence of fear; it is moving forward in spite of it.

Just Follow: Obey God, even with Fear.

He is God, and we are not. His ways are higher, more complex, and far better than ours. Even if you follow Him with fear and uncertainty, and even if you don't get the exact direction correctly (maybe He wanted you to take the left bridge instead of the right!), He understands. God is a good Father. He desires our obedience, even if it's not perfect. Not moving though, out of fear or laziness, will definitely not make Him happy. As a father myself, I understand this. If I asked our son, when younger, to clean his room before dinner, but he accidentally cleaned the living room instead, would I be upset? No, I'd smile and thank him for doing a great job, and we would have a wonderful dinner together. After dinner I would ask him to clean his room, and I would probably help him, because he showed obedience to me. However, if he ignored my request and did nothing, I would be disappointed and would discipline him. Disobedience in small things can lead to bigger issues. I want to trust him. Disobedience now could mean he may disobey when I warn him not to play in the street where there are cars and he could be hurt.

Trust God and obey, even if you're afraid. You will never be 100% certain you perfectly got the message; it does require trust and faith in Him. You never know what blessings are waiting on the other side of the fear. Do not miss out!

Fearing God: It is a Test, Pulling us Closer to God

I have seen where God has asked me to do something that just doesn't make sense. It is a test, will I follow, or will my fear of others or just laziness win? As I choose to *delight in the fear of the Lord*, I choose to follow obediently.

I was in Poland for a conference, most of the guests at the hotel were part of this Christian conference. The days are full, I was tired, I had gone to my room to pray, read my Bible and sleep. When sitting on my bed in pajamas with my Bible, I felt God telling me to go down to the lounge in the lobby and sit at a round table to read my Bible. *Really Lord? I am ready for bed and reading my Bible and You want me to go read my Bible at the lounge with others talking around me?* Yet I changed my clothes and went, not happy about it, but I obeyed. In the lounge area, sitting there alone, a Catholic Priest walked by. We started talking and I ended up being able to bless him in prayer, as he was anxious about where God wanted him to go after studying at the Vatican. Then a man who I had wanted to meet all week walked by and we talked for 15 minutes. Amazing!

It was a test from God. In fear I had obeyed. I was blessed. Others were blessed. I felt much closer to God and slept with a huge smile on my face that night. Obedience was more important to God than my Bible reading and prayer time that evening!

The fear of God is healthy. It motivates us to move. Sitting and not obeying, is not a good option. Dietrich Bonhoeffer was one of the few German pastors that fought against Hitler during World War II, ultimately, he was killed by the Nazis when he was taken prisoner. He said, *Silence in the face of evil is evil itself.*

My paraphrase is:
Inaction, in the face of evil, is the worst sort of evil.

Having God's favor rest on you is amazing, even if we follow Him in fear. May you delight greatly in the fear of the Lord!

Please ponder this:
_____

**God wants our active obedience,
not perfect obedience.**

Chapter 45

Run to the Fortress
(Day 33)

The Lord is my rock, my fortress and my deliverer;
my God is my rock, in whom I take refuge.
PSALM 18:2

Monday arrived, following the glorious Sunday when I had again surrendered my will to God, choosing to follow Him. It is important to note, surrendering your will, at least for me, is not *one and done*. It is a dynamic and evolving process where I think I have surrendered all to just follow Him, but then God will show me an area that is not under His control that also needs to be surrendered. This process will continue until I go to heaven, only then fully surrendered to Christ. Until then, step by step, polishing by polishing, God is slowly teaching me to follow Him more, and in the process, transforming me into being like Jesus *(Romans 8:28-29)*. I was still riding the wave of that incredible Sunday, filled with joy. Soon though, reality hit me, and the impact hurt. It came as I worked to book the flight two days out, for Wednesday, for the trip to Washington D.C. — the one I felt God had called me to make.

This was too much for my dear wife, and she pleaded with me not to go. I could feel the heartache in her words, and it shattered mine. She was hurting, as she felt overwhelmed with all the change in her life, difficulties in our extended family, and the uncertainty of things. It was too much and too fast, especially so soon after my three-week trip to Asia. Yet I couldn't ignore the undeniable calling I felt from God. His direction for me was unrelenting.

My wife, whom I love dearly, had not received any clear word from God about this. She was seeking His voice, but He remained silent. It was incredibly hard on her, and I knew that. She wept in the other room, as I in tears, booked the flight. My heart crushed with the weight of it all. It was only the fear of the Lord that motivated me to go. I didn't want to. I hated the concept even. I wasn't even sure what I would do for the four days. God had been preparing me the day before, testing me to see if I would follow Him, even when it hurt. It did hurt— piecing my heart. Worse though, I could see it crush my tender wife's heart, my bride and the most beautiful treasured part of my life. My choice to follow God was like my foot was stepping on my pink flower of a wife, deforming and hurting her so much. However, my fear of God was great, and in this fear I painfully and fearfully moved forward.

I just followed, dreading each step.

God was teaching me about the fear of the Lord *(Proverbs 1:7),* and showing me that He desires my obedience above all. He was my Lord, I was His servant, and I had vowed that to Him. I had promised to follow Him, no matter the cost, and I had no choice but to keep my word. Yet, amidst the sorrow and our tears, a joy began to slowly fill my heart. It made no sense to me. It actually made me angry. How could I feel joy in the midst of such cloudy gray sadness? I was confused, overwhelmed by the storm I saw with my eyes around me. Somehow, my heart began to overflow with joy, because I knew I was following His will, not my own. I had passed the test.

Fortress for My Heart

It reminded me of Psalm 18:2, where God is described as our impenetrable fortress:

The LORD is my rock, my fortress and my deliverer;
my God is my rock, in whom I take refuge

I desperately needed that security. God reminded me of a picture—a vision a friend had seen earlier in the year while I was in Poland. In it, my heart was held securely in a mountain fortress, perched beautifully on a rocky cliff with a spring-fed waterfall flowing from it. As the storm raged around me, I ran to that fortress, knowing my heart was protected there.

This same Monday, a friend prayed over me, and I felt God's presence in the words.

Lord, I pray that Craig would be the eyes and hands of Jesus. That he would see people through the eyes of Jesus – through their hurt, past all the layers of flesh. The closer we are to God, the more we see people as He sees them, and we begin to love them with His love. But in doing so, you will see with love, but you will also feel their pain, a burden that could overwhelm and drown you. But Jesus is with us. He carries that burden for us, and we become the conduit of His love to them. It's like gold dust flowing through us, with some of the residue remaining. Commingled pain with the gold. As we love like Him, we are transformed. As you look at someone with His eyes, His heart, it changes us to be like Him. Lord, make Craig surrendered to You, raise him up mighty in You. Lord, I see you pouring into Craig. May this DC trip be fruitful, big.

Those words shocked me, they were not the normal words of my friend. I felt they were directly from God to me. To encourage and instruct me. Following God is never a solitary journey, He is there. He speaks to us, and He uses others to speak His truth into our lives, like had beautifully just occurred. He is always there, a fortress we can run to. Following Him will bring pain—that's a certainty. As we read the Bible, especially in the life of Jesus, we see that pain and challenges are part of the path. Just following takes courage. Have hope, because the joy will ultimately outweigh the pain.

Weeping may remain for a night,
but joy comes in the morning.
Psalm 30:5

Focus on the joy that will come, not the pain.
Run to the Fortress. He is there.

Chapter 46

Commingled Joy and Pain
(Day 34)

'Lord, what about him?'

Jesus answered,
'If I want him to remain alive until I return,
what is that to you? You must follow me.'
JOHN 21:21-22

The morning was hard. My wife, seeking clarity, woke up early hoping to hear God's voice as to why I was leaving for Washington D.C. the next day. Seeing her tears again, rebroke my heart. Despite her prayers, God didn't give her an answer. I've learned that sometimes God explains, and sometimes He doesn't. The pain of seeing my wife not hear from God hurt me so much. I was asking God, *Why just me? Why don't You talk to her also? She is seeking You!* It is similar to what Jesus said to Peter in John 21:21-22, with Jesus basically saying *I get to pick, you do not.* I am sure Peter did not like hearing that, and I didn't either. Yet God is God, and He gets to pick, we do not.

Two Fingers and God's Hand

That morning, I went to help our elderly couple friends, Bob and Karen. Karen struggles with pain and on this day was barely able to walk. That morning, she clung to her walker as we slowly went to our car. She was anxious about her upcoming doctor's appointment, so we prayed together on the way there and in the lobby. With assistance, she made her way into the doctor's office. When I returned her to her home, she collapsed onto the couch, her husband Bob beside her. She was overcome with pain, fear, and an awful sense of separation from God's love. I sat beside her, reading Scripture and praying for her while holding her hand.

These last few years, I have learned to be still and listen to God more when praying. In that moment, I felt God's clear prompting to specifically place two fingers of my right hand on her chest, near her heart. I hesitated, and even asked, *why exactly two fingers?* I just sat there; eyes closed. It seemed awkward to reach across her and touch her chest in that way. I did not want to do it. I stayed quiet, asking God for confirmation. Then, I felt a nudge from God again, this time in a much more insistent tone, *do it!* I obeyed, reaching across her I gently placed my two fingers on her heart and prayed, that God would bless her heart and pour His love into her.

Suddenly, as I prayed, she grabbed my whole hand and pressed it tightly against her heart, weeping and weeping. I continued praying for her to feel God's love. After we were done, I sat there silently, we all were silent. It was hard for me to process all of this, because it was obvious she treasured my hand on her heart and me praying for her. I pondered why she had grabbed my whole hand with such force and pressing it down against her chest. She then told me, that in that moment, she had not heard my voice — it was Jesus' voice talking to her. She felt His touch through my touch, and it overwhelmed her, and she wanted so much more of His touch on her heart. I was moved and began to cry as well, realizing that God had used me as a vessel to pour His love directly into her hurting heart. Wow, and I in fear almost didn't obey. God had to give me strength to follow, but ultimately, I had to make a choice to follow or not, I am glad I followed. Without Him, we are weak, but He gives us the courage and strength needed. It was a glorious moment — for both of us, while Bob her husband sat there smiling next to her.

Family can be Challenging

Later, after spending time with Bob and Karen, I drove home. In addition to my sudden travel to Washington DC the next day, another punch was hitting my wife. I knew the afternoon would be emotionally difficult. Since my father passed away unexpectedly a few months ago, extended family relationships have become strained. My wife and I had heard and seen things that we never imagined we would. It had hurt us both severely, piercing my heart. I felt betrayed. I already had needed conversations about this with my family. She now had some things she needed to communicate, and bravely felt it was important to do so face-to-face. She had written a heartfelt letter and read it aloud to a family member that afternoon. It was not fully received as we had hoped, but neither was it met with hostility. I was so proud of my wife, as she had taken the step to forgive, starting the journey to her own healing and freedom.

Pain, joy, pain, it was a mixture of a day. Pain and joy commingled together. We rarely have all of one or the other. God's hand though was still guiding all of it.

sorrowful, yet always rejoicing
2CORINTHIANS 6:10

Chapter 47

Following is Hard
(Day 35)

Peace I leave with you; My peace I give you.
I do not give you as the world gives.
Do not let your hearts be troubled and do not be afraid.
JOHN 14:27

Wednesday morning 3:40 AM, I just could not sleep. My flight was later that evening at about midnight, making for a very long day ahead. My world was a storm of emotions, and my heart should have been crushed on this day. Yet surprisingly, my heart was at peace. I wrote in my journal:

Interesting Lord – I am at peace. I do not understand, but I believe. I have You, and that is enough. I hear You saying, 'Wait, follow Me.' Ha, and You promise that I will receive so much more. You are telling me to rejoice. I love You, Lord! Philippians 3:8 comes to mind: '...for whose sake I have lost all things.' I choose to follow You and know You better. I give it all up, to willingly follow You. I trust You with my dear bride. Show me how to love her well. Today, I go to DC alone – in more ways than just physically. I feel alone, I have only You, Lord. This is my cross, but I take it up gladly, as I love walking this path with You so much, even in the suffering, as Matthew 10:39 says: 'Whoever loses his life for My sake will find it.'

Despite the storm raging around me in the natural world, my heart remained calm and protected. I knew I was walking alone as I followed Him, but He was with me.

Just Follow

It was a night flight, and as I boarded, I was fortunate to have an empty seat next to me. The woman by the window, whose name I would later learn was Neala, covered her eyes and slept the entire flight. She was on her way home to Liberia. Little did I know that night, the reason God had specifically wanted me on that night flight was to meet and bless Neala, and for other events He would orchestrate in the coming days. I tried to sleep on the 4-hour flight, as it slowly carried me toward Washington D.C.

God is always working, even as we sleep. (or try to!)

The Protector of Israel will neither slumber nor sleep
PSALM 121:4

Chapter 48

Change of Path
(Day 36)

Trust in the Lord with all your heart,
and lean not on your own understanding;
in all your ways acknowledge Him
and He will make your paths straight.
PROVERBS 3:5-6

Years ago, I had spent hours meditating and pondering on these verses, which are so often used in Christian circles. Specifically, the word *acknowledge* kept drawing my attention. Looking it up, other synonyms are: submitted, recognize, see, agree, accept, or bow down. My key learning was that God wants us to surrender to His plans, to follow Him, that is what trust and leaning on Him is about. Then, He promises to give us a straight path. However, we must lean on and trust Him first! Note, God never said it would be an easy path, just a straight one, so we would know where He wanted us to go. I knew where He wanted me to go, I was in Washington D.C. Yet, all the plans I had, He was going to change. Today I would be tested, as I followed His path and not mine. In coming here, I clearly felt God wanted me to *only* spend time in prayer, no meetings planned, and I was set to obey and follow that command. He though is God, I am not, and He had other plans.

Early Thursday morning, I woke up slowly on the flight as we approached Washington D.C., not having slept much. I had a sense of God whispering to me, *You must follow Me*, as my mind replayed the tough departure from home. We landed just as dawn broke. While waiting to disembark, I started chatting with the woman seated next to me. Neala, originally from Liberia, was traveling there now to visit family. Liberia, she shared, was in turmoil. As we talked, I offered to pray for Liberia and her long journey, which would take 48 hours. Her face lit up with a smile, and she expressed how rare it was for someone to offer prayer, saying, *I would love for you to pray for me and my country!* Smiling, I was able to tell her that praying for people was actually something I get to do often, and enjoy doing it!

Prayer: Loving Deeply

We got off the flight, and went over by a quiet wall. I felt led to ask if there was anything personal she'd like me to pray for. She hesitated, just staring silently at me for what felt like forever. Then, in almost a trance, she shared that she and her husband dreamed of having a child. Recently, she had suffered two miscarriages, and a few months ago, she gave birth to a dead stillborn baby. I saw no tears in her eyes. My heart broke and I wept for her and her husband. I asked if I could pray for that also, and she softly replied, *of course — please do.* Holding her left arm I prayed slowly as my heart was in pain, for her and for her husband, so desiring God's touch of healing for them. I asked God to bless them with a child, and especially prayed for her husband, as I felt he had been devastated by this. When I had finished, tears had welled up in her eyes, and she hugged me tightly not letting go. She expressed how no one had ever prayed for her like that. I walked away, knowing she had hours of travel ahead, and that I would likely never see her again. God had used me from the moment my feet touched the ground by Washington D.C. to bless. It was beginning, the first of many people I would unexpectedly be blessed to pray with during this trip.

The Perfect Wrong Place

I had arrived at Dulles Airport, a place I'd never been, and further from Washington D.C. It felt like the wrong place to be. On every other trip, I always traveled to the closer airport to Washington D.C., as the Dulles Airport is a 1-hour subway ride to town. As I walked to the subway, I got a sudden text from a friend in D.C. He asked if he could connect me with Brittany, a former Presidential Appointee, who was highly connected in the government. We were introduced via text as I was already traveling on the subway, and she suggested a quick meeting at a local mall by her home. I realized I was only three subway stops away from where she wanted to meet—perfect timing! Now I knew why God had wanted me at Dulles Airport. The subway went right by the mall, allowing us to meet that morning.

On the subway, I called my friend Raymond, who had opened the door for me to attend the Lausanne Conference in Korea. I gave him an update from the conference and thanked him for giving me the chance to attend. We prayed for the upcoming meeting with Brittany. After arriving at the shopping mall where we were to meet, I freshened up in the bathroom to try and appear as if I had not been on a flight all night. I changed my shirt and shoes, putting on dress shoes. Little did I realize at the time, but I forgot to repack my running shoes and left them there in the bathroom at the mall, but more on that later. After changing, had a light breakfast and sat there on the patio outside reflecting, praying and reading my Bible. God already was orchestrating meetings with people, different from my plans!

Miraculous Political Connections – and Friends

I texted Alex, my friend stuck at the airport in South Korea, who God is raising up to pray. I asked him if he could pray for my meeting with Brittany. It's something I've learned: when you ask someone to pray for you, it shows how much you value them, and you both get to share in the blessings when God moves. I was able to call him, and we prayed over the phone. Just as Alex finished praying, a woman approached, still on her phone, it was Brittany. We greeted each other and headed inside for coffee. Over the next two hours she shared her remarkable journey into a senior role within the U.S. government. She even gave me a book to read. Before parting ways, I prayed for her, her husband, children and that God would direct her next step. What added to the feeling of God orchestrating things, was that the person who she was talking to on her phone when we met, I would be meeting with in person the very next day. Despite being strangers at first, it was clear that through the Holy Spirit, we were united, a team on a common mission to impact the United States with the love and values of God.

After my meeting with Brittany, I boarded the subway and quickly arrived near the White House in Washington DC. Although the day was beautiful, there was a dark heavy spiritual atmosphere, as if a thick wet gray blanket covered the entire area. God though reminded me to pray only in a very specific way, to:

Rejoice in the victory and the gift you will receive.

White House – Spiritual Heaviness

Normally, I would have prayed for the heaviness to lift and for God's power to fill the place, but instead I simply followed instructions. So, I was praising Him for the victory of what He has done, what He is doing, and what He will do. Also, with much curiosity I thought about the mysterious gift He had promised.

Unexpectedly, I met with my friend Samuel, who works in DC and previously served as a senior Presidential Appointee. We hadn't seen each other in over a year, so it was great to reconnect. After our conversation, I prayed for him, and to my surprise, he offered to pray for me as well. This rarely happens, someone desiring to also pray for me. I welcomed it warmly, lifting my hands in gratitude for how God was unexpectedly blessing my time in D.C.

Exact Answer to Prayer

After leaving Samuel, I received a text message and then got on the phone with Jala, from Uganda, who I had met in Korea at the Lausanne Conference. She was heading to a speaking engagement and told me she needed to talk. Jala shared how God had called her to attend a conference in Ghana, even though she didn't have the money for the trip. She mentioned that she had received a text from me, where I had prayed for God to provide for all of her and her husband's needs. She and her husband read the text message together and prayed specifically for the $697 needed for her round-trip plane ticket. She called to tell me that on the very same day, she received a check for exactly $697. I was ecstatic! Together, we praised God for hearing our prayers and answering them so specifically.

Lots of Roommates

With this joy bouncing in my heart, I made the 25-minute walk to the hostel where I was staying for the night. Given the last-minute nature of the trip and the upcoming U.S. presidential election, the hotels were quite expensive. The hostel was far more affordable. For those unfamiliar with hostels, they are places where you share a room with strangers, often with four to ten people sleeping on bunk beds in a common room. Bathrooms are communal and located down the hall for everyone to use. I hadn't stayed in a hostel in over 35 years, not since I was a college graduate backpacking through Europe. A hostel was not my first pick, but I was guessing God had a plan in this somehow. I wasn't sure what to expect; it felt like another adventure on top of the one I was already on.

Checking into the hostel was easy, and I put my things on the bed and headed out again, this time to the White House area to pray.

Chapter 49

Favor and Connections
(Day 36-continued)

We fix our eyes not on what is seen,
but on what is unseen.
For what is seen is temporary,
but what is unseen is eternal.
2 CORINTHIANS 4:18

L ate Thursday afternoon, my first day in Washington D. C.
and I had not really slept much on the flight, so was feeling
tired. Walking the 20 minutes to Lafayette Park, near the White
House, I sat on a bench and prayed. It felt different this time as
compared to other trips here, heavy, oppressive, full of fear.
There were security barricades everywhere, and a large stage
was being constructed. People speculated it was for the
inauguration, but that was still months away. Others told me it
was being done as a preventative measure to protect the area
from potential unrest during the election. As I sat there, I prayed
as God had instructed, thanking Him for the victory He would
bring, even though I couldn't see it. I realized that,
rejoicing in a promise that is yet unseen is very hard!

It was much harder than asking for something specific, but I
smiled, realizing this was exactly why God was telling me to
rejoice, it was increasing my trust and faith in Him. The verse
from 2 Corinthians 4:18 came to mind: *So, we fix our eyes not on
what is seen, but on what is unseen. For what is seen is temporary, but
what is unseen is eternal.* The verse didn't say how hard it is to
actually do it! I was finding out.

Prayer for Favor and Connections

I didn't have much time to pray, as I wanted to attend a prayer service at National Community Church, where Mark Batterson is the lead pastor. I took the subway and while walking to the church, memories from my previous visit flooded back. Almost exactly two years earlier, I had been to this church on a trip with my family. It had been planned just before learning that my job at Intel would be eliminated. It felt like a leap of faith to take it, at the time, but God used it powerfully. I had briefly met Mark in the lobby, and he invited me to a prayer meeting later in the week, where God led me to read aloud from Luke 1:46-55 – the Magnificat, Mary's prayer of praise. Mark then walked over, placed his hand on my left shoulder and prayed for me, asking God to grant me *favor and connections* as I transitioned out of Intel into this new chapter. Now, two years later, I was returning, filled with favor and connected to people from around the world.

I Surrender All

During the prayer meeting at the church, the song *I Surrender All* played, which felt perfectly fitting:

> *All to Jesus, I surrender.*
> *All to Him, I freely give.*
> *I will ever love and trust Him.*
> *In His presence daily live.*

It was the big lesson God had been teaching me these two years. I had a heavy matter on my heart, this calling from God. As I prayed, I sensed God calling me again to surrender all and to obey Him. He reassured me that I was on the correct path. I wanted an easier path, a path that would be more conformed to how others do things. It hurts to even write this, as in Romans 12:2 the Bible tells us specifically, *Do not be conformed to the patterns of this world,* and there I was asking God to give me a normal conforming path to what the world would expect. I was not wanting to follow God! He clearly told me that night in the church, *No – I have called you to this.* The verse in Hebrews 5:4 came to mind when God called Aaron to be a priest saying, *No one takes this honor upon himself; he must be called by God.* I did feel honored, I knew I was called by God, but there was still fear in following Him on this path. I felt I needed more confirmation, so I asked for it. It would happen in minutes. Soon after this dialog with God, I felt prompted by Him to leave the service early and wait in the lobby, which was unusual, but this sort of unexpected change is not unprecedented in my journey with God. It feels like it is more normal than abnormal! It reminded me of an event a few months prior, one morning as I was having an amazing time with God on the couch. God had told me that day to immediately stop reading my Bible and to stop praying and instead to go watch a training video. What?!?! That was all quite confusing to me, but I obeyed. I would have never guessed God would want me to pray and read the Bible less! About 30 minutes into the video, I was amazed to see Pam, a person that I actually was going to have a meeting with two hours later. What?!?! It was perfect timing to watch that training video. Do not try to put God and His ways in a box. Even if God may ask you to do things that do not make sense, you must follow Him.

Praying for a Chaplain and Prisoners

So, I went to the church lobby. I noticed a woman pacing back and forth. I introduced myself and learned her name was Sharon, a military chaplain overwhelmed with stress from a big software project at work and it sounded like there were challenges in her marriage. For years I worked at implementing large software systems so we talked about that for a while. I asked if I could pray for her, and though surprised at first, she smiled and agreed. I asked her to cup her hands as if receiving something, a practice I find helpful when praying with others. As I prayed, tears flowed, and I sensed that healing had begun in her heart, in her marriage and that her job would not overwhelm her. After the final amen, she looked at me with tears in her eyes, thanking me. She just sat there, in shock that a complete stranger had cared enough to see her, come to her and to pray.

Next was a video call with Alex from the Korean airport. It would be with Alex and a new friend of his named Claire from

Rwanda. Both felt like prisoners there. About a week ago I had sent him an audio prayer, I had asked for God to show Alex a person at the airport that he could bless and pray for. He had taken the prayer to heart and went to pray in the same prayer chapel where we had met. As he was praying, a woman's face and her name kept appearing in his mind. It was Claire, who had been living there at the airport for a year. She was one of 15 women who were there at the airport, along with the 25 men that were also stuck there. Alex did not know her well, so he asked God for a sign – specifically that she would see him that day, and that she would walk up to him to talk. About an hour later, this was exactly what happened and Alex was beyond surprised. At that point, even though he felt awkward, he felt he had to ask her to pray, as God had done His part of the deal. They prayed together that day, in the same prayer chapel where I had originally met Alex. Today I would meet her on this video call, and I would pray for her. Alex had already told her all about me. We had the chance to meet and I was blessed to pray for her. She had likely not received prayer for the year she had been stuck there at the airport. God's timing is always perfect. Later that night she had a mental and physical breakdown. The prayer time and feeling God's love was absolutely God's way to protect her, as she could have died that night. A week later, she returned to Rwanda. When God calls, we need to obey. Our refusal to obey could dramatically impact others.

Smiling from all that had occurred at the church prayer meeting and in the lobby, I took a taxi back to the hostel. I had a meaningful conversation with the driver, who allowed me to pray for him before I got out. He honked and waved as he drove off, and I went to my room. As I prepared for bed, it was then that I realized I had left my running shoes in the bathroom at the mall near the airport. I'd have to walk around the city in dress shoes the next day, thousands of steps. I had never lost my shoes in traveling! This all made me laugh, knowing that somehow, even this would become part of God's plan.

Drifting off to sleep, surrounded by four strangers from around the world, I marveled at the mystery of God's ways. None of the day had gone according to my plans, but following Him had been much better than anything I could have imagined. I felt like I was soaking in:

God's Favor and Connections

Chapter 50

God's Promise
(Day 37)

*being absolutely convinced
that God would do what He had promised*
ROMANS 4:21

Sunrise and I was up. My mind wakes up fast, and I was already pondering, *God had also promised me a gift, would I better understand that today?* I quietly slipped out of my hostel room, careful not to disturb my sleeping roommates. I had lost my running shoes and wondered how I was going to manage walking seven laps around the White House in dress shoes. Stopping at a nearby pharmacy, I picked up some insoles, trimming them to size with a pair of store scissors, as the cashier watched and smiled. With that, I was off—ready to circle the White House, trusting in how God wanted me to pray:
Rejoice in the victory and the gift I will give you.

I had an idea of what the victory might be, as I assumed it was likely tied to the upcoming U.S. presidential election. As for the *gift*, that was a mystery, but I was hoping it was the desk in the Eisenhower Executive Office Building (EEOB) that God had promised me four years ago. The EEOB is a large building adjacent to the White House, housing the President's key staff, advisors and government leaders.

Washington D.C. Prayer – Four Years Earlier

To understand this promise, we need to go back four years earlier. This perspective will give you background on not just this promise of a desk, but how God has been leading me over the years. These trips to Asia and to Washington D.C. were not unprecedented, having followed God many times, including traveling. Washington D.C. is a very special place to me personally, having been called to this specific city to pray many times over the years. Nearly to the day four years prior, God called me to travel to Washington D.C., ahead of the 2020 presidential election to pray for the nation. It was September 26, 2020, and two major prayer events were happening. One was led by Franklin Graham, and another took place right on the National Mall in front of the Capitol. At sunrise that morning, I went to the U.S. Supreme Court, feeling led to pray fervently against the evil of abortion and asking God to raise up court justices who would protect life and lead the nation in righteous ways.

As I finished praying at the Supreme Court by the main door, I noticed a number of news crews setting up cameras, and police putting up barricades. Curious, I asked one of the reporters what was going on, and they told me that the President was expected to announce a Supreme Court nominee later that day. I was amazed at God's timing. Walking around the Capitol, I continued to pray, specifically that there would be no rioting or violent protests following the announcement.

That day was spent all afternoon and into the evening at the prayer rallies on the large Washington Mall. They were powerful events, with the final song being performed by Michael W. Smith. As he sang the song *Let it Rain*, a light drizzle began, the first rain of the day — a beautiful, gentle reminder of God's presence. I knelt in the wet grass, overcome, praising God and praying for the nation.

When the rally ended, it was dark and the rain intensified. Despite the downpour, I was drawn to the Capitol to see if there had been any protests in response to the nomination. I heard it was announced that morning, as the prayer gatherings were occurring on the other side of the Capitol building. The judge nominated was known for her strong pro-life stance against abortion, and like the police, I assumed that would have triggered significant rioting.

As I approached the Capitol, I saw a strange sight. A group of about 100 bicyclists, covered in lights, moved through the pouring rain, talking among themselves. It felt eerie, sinister, as their voices and laughter echoed in the deserted street through the driving rain. I prayed for protection as I crossed in front of them on the crosswalk. I felt led to pray that they would not cross that crosswalk, that God would erect an invisible barrier, keeping them from getting closer to the Capitol. Despite there being no traffic, and it being a stop sign and not a stoplight, they remained frozen in place as I passed, all their eyes watching me. That motivated me to walk fast as I prayed! Walking away, I glanced back—astonished to see that they still hadn't moved, frozen there at the crosswalk. It was as if they were held back by some unseen force.

Rounding the Capitol, now on the eastern side by the Supreme Court building, I was stunned by the calm that greeted me. It was peaceful, quiet, dark with not a single person in sight. Only a lone security officer stood by the barricades. I approached her, asking how the protests had gone. She was wide-eyed, saying that security had been bracing for large potentially violent demonstrations, but in the end, only about a dozen people showed up that afternoon. She said they talked among themselves, then left without incident. The officer remarked how unusual it was, as protests had followed every other Supreme Court appointment, especially under President Trump. Smiling, I mentioned the prayer rally on the other side of the Capitol and how I had prayed for peace earlier that morning, exactly where she was now standing. She looked at me, obviously didn't know what to say, and simply said, *thanks*.

The Promise of a Desk

It was the next two days during that amazing trip that directly connected to God's promise of a desk. On Sunday, September 27th, God called me to the Washington Monument to spend the entire evening and late into the night praying for the nation. During those hours, I was convicted of the many sins of the country, and felt there was one sin in particular that grieved God more than all the others, it was a heavy, horrible, dark night of praying. I had a hard time sleeping when I finally returned to my hotel after midnight.

The following day, Monday, September 28th, 2020, I was sitting on a bench outside the White House praying and enjoying the perfect weather. God clearly talked to me as I was staring at the White House and the EEOB office building next to it. He said He was going to give me a desk in the EEOB, where the Presidential staff and advisors work. That surprised me, and I remember that moment very well, as I had not been praying or asking for that at all. It was God's call on my life, and at some point, it would be fulfilled. What is interesting to note, is that to the day, exactly 2 years after this event, I would hear that my job at Intel had been eliminated. God orchestrates all the details! May we keep our eyes open to see them.

Walking Time

Now, almost exactly four years later, I was in Washington D.C. in October, once again walking around the White House. Each time I circled it, I caught a glimpse of the EEOB and was reminded of God's promise. When would this be fulfilled? I did not know, but I was expecting it would be soon as God always does what He has promised.

...if my people, who are called by my name,
will humble themselves and pray and seek my face and turn
from their wicked ways, then I will hear from heaven, and I
will forgive their sin and will heal their land.
2 CHRONICLES 7:14

Seven Times and $100 (Day 37-continued)

I will give you every place where you set your foot
JOSHUA 1:3

Does location matter for prayer? I have heard people, even a senior religious leader say, *you can pray and be with God anywhere, location doesn't matter.* I would call that response a half-truth, dangerously similar to what the serpent told Eve to deceive her, which created the first sin. We have to be discerning, we can pray anywhere of course, but location can also be of critical importance. All of it depends on what God is doing, we just have to follow. God gave this promise to Joshua that where he would walk, it would be given to him. I felt as though God had extended that promise to me as well. This verse had been inscribed on the floor of the prayer room at Mark Batterson's church two years prior, a perfect reminder as I circled the White House. This filled my mind as I walked around the White House, completing seven laps — over 20,000 steps and 10 miles(16km). I reached out to a few friends to pray as I walked. The first was Pedro, my friend from Costa Rica, now the global Christian leader at Intel. I had prayed with him outside the White House at the exact spot where I was now walking, on four different occasions — twice in person and twice over the phone. It was God's perfect timing, again, that Pedro was available to pray with me. It was a powerful time as we prayed over the country.

Next, I called my prayer friends Kirsten and Heesung, with whom I pray weekly. Kirsten was able to answer the call and I prayed with her. She prayed for God's power to descend as I continued walking, rejoicing on the green lawn of the Ellipse between the White House and the Washington Monument. The usual sidewalk closer to the White House was closed for a period, requiring me to walk further to do the laps, which seemed frustrating at the time. In hindsight, I see it was part of God's plan. A week later, this was the very spot on the grass where Vice President Kamala Harris would deliver her final formal speech before the election. What initially seemed like an inconvenience, adding more steps, placed me right where I needed to be when praying. Amen!

Pain under the Leaves

After finishing the seven laps, which took 3 hours, I sat down on a bench, reflecting with tired feet and a heart full of joy. I believed God had promised me a gift — I was very curious what it could be. It was a beautiful Fall Day there in Lafayette Park looking at the White House. I called my wife to share my joy. She missed me profoundly and was heartbroken. As I prayed for her, I felt the pain too. The joy I had just experienced was now mixed with sorrow. It was a moment of victory and deep pain, bittersweet, as I sat there on the bench with the red fall leaves falling around me.

Surprise Detour

It was now time to eat, so I went to our favorite breakfast spot in Washington D.C. — the Corner Bakery, near the White House. I enjoyed scrambled eggs, cinnamon roll French toast, and bacon, which tasted even better as I had been fasting that morning during the walk. I felt grateful for the meal and took a moment to chat with the manager, even snapping a selfie with him, which made him laugh and smile. It reminded me how a simple thank you and chat can change the trajectory of someone's day. Afterward, I returned to the hostel, changed into more formal clothes, and headed to an afternoon coffee meeting, with someone from the Heritage Foundation who had been in a senior government role. Arriving early to the coffee spot, I took a quick detour to visit the Heritage Foundation building. They had heightened security, including metal detectors and armed guards, because of many violent threats related to their Project 2025 program.

Inside, I met Ruth the receptionist, originally from Kenya. When she asked what brought me to Washington D.C., I told her I was there to pray. Her eyes lit up, and she shared that she too, had been called by God to pray. Having driven to different states across the country just to pray. I was amazed, as I rarely meet others with a similar calling, we agreed to talk more. Now it was time to meet the two men for coffee, both had worked in senior roles under President Trump during his first term.

I had coffee with them, and quickly learned how the government distributes billions of dollars of aid annually to various nations and organizations. It was fascinating to hear the stories and passion for ensuring that the money went to the right places—as there is corruption and inefficiencies that need to be guarded against. They were interested in my background in finance, contracts, and deal-making, and we had a great conversation about the importance of industry experience in government. We exchanged contact information.

A Blessing: Praying Jewish Friend

After coffee, I went back to the Heritage Foundation to catch up with Ruth. It was perfect timing, as she was on her break, so we sat down in the courtyard to chat. Ruth shared her story with me. She had grown up Christian, but recently felt that God was calling her to become a Jew. She converted recently to be a Jew, and she fully believes that Jesus is the Messiah, being God. When I asked if she was a Messianic Jew, she said she wasn't— just a Jew who believes Jesus is the Messiah. She mentioned that her Rabbi knew about this and was fine with it, which amazed me. During my time in Jerusalem, I had spoken with Orthodox Rabbis who definitely wouldn't have accepted that kind of belief. At the end of our talk, I offered to pray for her, and it was very special. As I prayed, I felt led to pray for her to get married. She later shared that as I was praying, she saw a vision of herself in a short-sleeved white dress with a veil, getting married. It was a blessed moment.

The Gift

Ruth loves to pray, as I do. We agreed to meet the next day, Saturday, to pray for the nation at the Washington Monument. As I was getting ready to leave the Heritage Foundation, she was back at her post at the receptionist's desk. We had a final chat, then she suddenly said, *put out your hand.* I did, and she placed a crumpled-up piece of paper in my hand, and she closed my fingers around it. Telling me it was for me, a gift. When I opened it, I was stunned — it was a $100 bill! I had no idea why Ruth had given it to me. She smiled and explained that she would miss the Jewish holiday, which would end at sundown on Friday. During this holiday, people hold the Jewish Torah and dance with joy. She had planned to give the $100 at the synagogue, but instead, she gave it to me, saying, *you are a man of God, traveling, blessing people, ministering, and without pay as you cover all your own costs. You need to be paid.* I was speechless, carefully unfolding and smoothing this priceless gift and putting it in my wallet. I haven't spent it, and I never will. It was a gift from God, given to me from His servant from Kenya, a lady named Ruth. It was the first time anyone had given me money for traveling and ministering.

I felt God smile, reminding me of His promise to provide for me, and to give me a gift. Having commanded me to pray, *Rejoice in the victory and the gift I will give you.* On the same day I walked around the White House rejoicing, God decided to give me this surprise gift. I had been blessed in so many ways through Ruth. As I left, I reflected on her name — Ruth. I couldn't help but think of the biblical story of Ruth and Boaz, a beautiful, romantic story of faith in following God. Boaz had given up a sandal to claim Ruth as his bride. It struck me, that I too, had given something up — my running shoes, forgotten in that restroom when I first arrived. I laughed as I thought of it, but it did feel like it was somehow a symbolic act, as if God was saying I had to give up something small to claim a far greater gift there in Washington D.C.

The $100 bill, is a treasure in my office. A gift from the nations, from a wonderful Kenyan sister in Christ named Ruth who God strategically placed in Washington D.C. to pray and bless. God reminded me of a prayer a friend from Canada once prayed over me, that I would receive the wealth of nations. God's promises are true, and He uses unexpected ways to fulfill them!

Rejoice in the victory and the gift I will give you.

Chapter 52

Praying for the Nation
(Day 38)

I urge, then, first of all, that petitions, prayers,
intercession and thanksgiving be made for all people —
for kings and all those in authority
1 TIMOTHY 2:1-2

Breakfast again at the same Corner Bakery and I ate the same thing, workers there were recognizing me and knew what I wanted, just smiling at me as I ordered. I had an incredible phone conversation with David. We met just a few months ago at church and quickly became friends. Like me, David has traveled extensively and shares a passion for both the nations and the United States. He leads the space program at a major public university and is frequently invited to speak with global leaders, technologists, and governments around the world. As I enjoyed my breakfast, over the phone we discussed how it seemed that God was orchestrating various groups — government, private industry, churches, technologists, and more — to unite, to assist Christians to come together to help all the people in the world. It was a profound conversation to have as I watched a parade of large shiny black SUVs arrive outside my window as I peered down at the street, each carrying dignitaries and their security details. In that moment, I felt strongly that God was reminding me that I was called to impact nations, and how Courageous Third has a key part in the middle of this. This puzzle God was having me put together was slowly taking shape.

PRAY

After breakfast I took a leisurely walk to the Washington Monument. It was a beautiful day. I wore my white t-shirt with the word *PRAY* boldly printed in black, a gift from Matt, one of the founders of PRAY.COM, whom I met at a conference in Washington D.C. a few years prior. Matt and I had prayed at the Washington Monument together late one night, so I sent him a selfie wearing the shirt. Having visited the monument countless times during my trips here, always to pray—at dawn, noon, dusk, and even in the dead of night—it felt like I was returning home. Taking my time, as I always do, walking around the 50 flagpoles praying for each state in turn. On this perfect blue-sky day as I circled the monument, I could see the Lincoln Memorial, the Capitol, and the White House in the distance. I eventually sat on one of the many large white marble benches, facing the White House, waiting for Ruth to join me for prayer.

We are the Bride of Christ

When she arrived, we asked God for guidance, and she felt led to read sections from Hosea 2:19-23. It was especially meaningful, as Ruth is a Jew.

> *I will make you my wife forever, showing you righteousness and justice, unfailing love and compassion. I will be faithful to you and make you mine, and you will finally know me as the LORD... I will plant her for myself in the land; I will show love to those I called 'Not loved.' And to those I called 'Not my people,' I will say, 'Now you are my people.' And they will reply, 'You are our God!'"*

As we read, I felt God speaking to me. Hosea's wife had not loved him or been faithful, much like how the United States has strayed from the Lord in some areas. Yet, God says, *I will plant her for myself in the land*. This felt like a personal message—that God was planting me in Washington D.C., to be used for His purposes. I reflected on the miraculous events of the past two years in places like Rome, Israel, Poland, Korea and China. My name, Craig, is of Scottish origin and means *rocky outcropping*, so basically my name, like Peter, means *rock*. Thinking about Matthew 16, where Jesus renames Simon as Peter. Jesus states that on this rock He will build His church, and God will give the keys to the kingdom of heaven and earth. I journaled my thoughts:

Like in Hosea's passage, I and all believers are the bride of Christ. God gave me His heart of love earlier in the year – His merciful love for people. Like Peter, God revealed a key part of His character to me, His merciful heart of love for all. For me to somehow use this key of love, to build up, unite, connect and inspire His Church.

Afterward, leaving the monument, we pausing by the US Commerce Department building to pray. My mind was full of thoughts and reflections. While walking to the hostel, visited the National Museum of Women in the Arts. Amazingly appropriate, I thought, as my mind was processing how God in these verses in Hosea calls us to a wedding, to be His bride. The museum was fascinating to see – the art was by and about women. The artwork conveyed a palpable sense of hurt, frustration, and anger at men. There was much pain mixed with joy. What was striking though, was that in the museum's beautiful lobby, they were preparing for a wedding. It was symbolic – a reminder that despite the struggles women face and anger towards men, many women still dream of love and marriage. Reflecting on this and the Hosea passage, I felt God's call again to uplift and encourage women.

Unexpected Hostel Friends

I returned to the hostel late that evening. I had a small piece of leftover bread I would eat for dinner, so I went to the common area kitchen to eat. As I sat down, I noticed a group of young people in their 20s, sitting a few feet from one other, each lost in their phone, sitting in silence. No interaction, no dialog. Soon, I was joined in the common kitchen area by two women around my age, also there to eat. One was from the United Kingdom, originally coming from Taiwan, and the other was from Turkey. Both were professors with PhDs in their area of discipline. The woman from the UK was studying democracy, particularly observing the phenomenon of Donald Trump's presidency. She was fascinated, saying, *we've never seen anything like what Trump is doing!* She was excitedly planning to attend a Trump rally in New York the next day. Esmeray, had been sent by the Turkish government to learn about incorporating diversity, equity, and inclusion (DEI) into their educational system, particularly in relation to refugees and women, who face significant challenges in Turkish society. Hearing about the struggles of women once again moved me. We shared stories, and she showed me photos of her travels, family, and life.

I met one of my hostel roommates. A young man named Andy, who was finishing up his PhD in Computer Science. Our oldest son was at this exact time applying for PhD programs in Computer Science, so I talked with Andy extensively. Later, I connected Andy up with our son, and he gave our son invaluable advice on how to best apply for PhD programs! Now I felt I knew why God wanted me in this hostel, not just to save some money, but to meet Andy.

In the room, I hoped that of my 5 roommates, the man above me that snored had checked out. He had not. Lying in the bunk bed, literally under his snoring, I reflected on the day — from the delicious cinnamon French toast and uplifting conversation with David in the morning, praying in the afternoon, to meeting a Turkish professor in the evening and surprisingly meeting Andy. What a full and blessed day. Tomorrow, I would leave D.C. It was my last full day, and in spite of the snoring of the man above me, I slept well.

Pray for Your Nation

Do you see yourself as the greatly loved bride of Christ? You are. A bride cares about what her husband cares about, that includes the nation you live in. I have a daily habit for over 25 years, of putting out an American flag at our home. Every time I touch it; I pray for the nation. God commands us to pray for our leaders.

Pray for your nation and its leaders.

I urge then, first of all, that petitions, prayers, intercession and thanksgiving... for kings and all those in authority
1 TIMOTHY 2:1-2

Chapter 53

Bookended in Power
(Day 39)

Would you be free from the burden of sin?
There's power in the blood, power in the blood;
Would you over evil a victory win?
There's wonderful power in the blood.
HYMN – POWER IN THE BLOOD

This morning I woke up well before sunrise, and I walked to the White House one last time to pray before leaving, lifting up a prayer of thanksgiving for the victory and for the gift I had received from Ruth. I stood there by the large EEOB building next to the White House, wondering when God would fulfill His promise of the desk, and how the Courageous Third platform would fit into all of this. Also, walking by an apartment building praying my wife and I would have a place in it. For the third day in a row, I went to the same Corner Bakery café and enjoyed the exact same breakfast, greeted by the same smiling manager who expected my same order. If it is good, why change it! In my quiet time there with God, I was filled with joy. Afterward, I returned to the hostel, checked out, and eagerly awaited Ruth, who was picking me up to drive us to her church.

As we drove, I realized Ruth hadn't been to this Pentecostal church for over a year. It wasn't her regular place of worship, yet I felt God whisper, *get ready for something good!* She happily showed me the car God had blessed her with; it had well over 300,000 miles on it, and it drove very well. Arriving at this old church camp in the country, it felt like stepping back 50 years in time. Walking into the simple white wooden church building, you could feel God's presence. Ruth introduced me to an elderly woman who looked like was in her 90s. She was tiny, but her love was huge—she pulled me down close, kissed my cheek, and welcomed me warmly. Wow, what love!

Power in the Blood – the Closing Bookend

Inside, the band was playing, people were clapping, dancing, and celebrating with a joy that couldn't be contained by the four walls. The church was 90% African Americans, and it was unlike anything I'd ever experienced—pure joy! The women up front sang as the men in the band played. Soon they launched into a very lively version of the hymn *Power in the Blood*. I couldn't believe it! This was the same hymn I had heard on my first day in Korea, about 40 days prior. Now, here I was, on my last day in Washington D.C. hearing it again. My mind was racing—what were the odds? This same song, bookending this 40-day journey, both times proclaiming God's power over evil. The last verse touched me.

> *Would you **do service** for Jesus, your King?*
> *There's power in the blood, power in the blood;*
> *Would you **live daily His praises to sing?***
> *There's wonderful power in the blood.*

It hit me profoundly, personally. I had done service for Jesus my King, traveling the world at His call and ministering to people from so many nations. Now I was wrapping up this trip to Washington D.C. where I had been commanded to rejoice, to praise Him. How appropriate to sing this on this final day!

I found myself at the front, praising God, overwhelmed with joy. As I knelt in worship, they formed a joyful procession circling the entire sanctuary, dancing and singing *Power in the Blood* with radiant delight! My heart was so full it felt like it might burst. With hands lifted high and tears streaming down my face, I praised God for His overwhelming goodness. 40 days prior I had heard this same hymn while kneeling at the front, in South Korea on Prayer Mountain sung in Korean. Realizing the full control God has over everything, even the church music selections, made me laugh inside and also feel so at peace - as God is in control, I can rest as I just follow.

As I reflected on all this, I was in awe of the diversity in the global Body of Christ. Seeing it on three continents just this year. Six months prior, I had been in Poland, spending hours in silent prayer in a Catholic chapel, hearing beautiful a cappella singing surrounded by nuns. It was meditative, and it filled my heart with peace, I could clearly hear God speak, and it is where Jesus gave me His heart. Then, just a few weeks ago, I had been at the Lausanne Conference in Korea with thousands of people from 180 nations, praising God with incredible music, lights, and everything ultra-professional with over 5000 people all praising God. Then in China with just 10 others meeting in a basement room turned church, with a piano and acoustic guitar, listening to Chinese praise music. Now, here I was, by Washington D.C., in a Black Pentecostal church, where the joy was palpable, the dancing was overflowing with God's glory, and my heart was exploding with gratitude. The beauty in the diversity of the Christian faith is vast and profound. It is such a treasure.

Soldier, Athlete, and Farmer

The sermon that day was based on 2 Timothy 2:3-7, the last book Paul wrote before his execution in Rome. Nearly two years earlier, I had visited the cold, dark, damp, Mamertine prison where Paul was held and had written 2 Timothy shortly before being executed. I had also visited the site where he was beheaded, and on that day, I had asked God to fill me with His power while kneeling in the spot where Paul the Apostle had died. God's response was quick and unexpected: *I will make you utterly weak and dependent on Me, and then I will give you My power.* At the time, that message had hurt a lot, crushing me. Now, nearly 2 years later, I understood. God needed to give me His loving heart, and to teach me how to follow. His love I have learned is what gives us the best life, and unleashes His power in us, pouring out His love to those around us. He had been steadily teaching me to rely on Him and on others for everything, to just follow.

The Pastor spoke about suffering and following Christ, drawing from these verses, 2 Timothy 2:3-7:

*Join with me in **suffering**, like a good soldier of Christ Jesus. No one serving as a **soldier** gets entangled in civilian affairs, but rather tries to please his commanding officer. Similarly, anyone who competes as an **athlete** does not receive the victor's crown except by competing according to the rules. The hardworking **farmer** should be the first to receive a share of the crops. Reflect on what I am saying, for the Lord will give you insight into all this.*

The message challenged me. I should expect to **suffer**. Then as a **soldier** I am called to achieve an objective, and I must push forward, overcoming every obstacle, focused 100% on pleasing my commanding officer, God. Pushing away distractions, and that my life will not look like others, the civilians. As an **athlete**, there are biblical principles, rules, that we must obey and follow. There are some rules that apply to all, but there are also unique rules that may apply individually to each of us. I must follow both the overarching ones and the unique ones God has called me to, realizing the individual rules He put on me may be different from those He puts on others. As a **farmer,** following God is not easy; it requires hard work, endurance, discipline, suffering, and there is a cost.

The Pastor closed with a powerful statement:
If you know what to do, but do not do it, that is sin.

God has made His will extremely clear to me; any deviation from that is sin and disobedience to God. He wants me to obey and love people deeply. A great fear of God is in my heart. I will not stand before God someday, alone in His mighty presence, and have the King of Kings look me in the eye, and ask me why I did not fully follow. I have no other choice, I must follow.

The Spear: Women and Men

Driving to the airport, I reflected on the service, the building alive with dancing and joyful singing. Joy unleashed! The band was made up entirely of men, while four women led the singing. The women also formed the majority of those dancing joyfully in the church. A vivid image came to my mind: it was as if God's

Body, His Church, was a spear with men and women each playing their unique roles. Women were the weighted tip of the spear, a powerful and dangerous part. Yet, without the long shaft of the spear — the men — the spearhead would be ineffective. The shaft could be somewhat useful without the spearhead, but when combined with the spearhead it is 100x more effective. Only united together, the men and women, could the unified spear accomplish its purpose. I felt that God was showing me how it is men's role to be the force and power to propel the spearhead forward, with the spearhead then naturally accomplishing what it was designed to do. Women innately, with God's most powerful attribute of love contained in their hearts, will change the world. Yet, it takes men to unleash and drive forward this powerful gift of love embodied in women. Close teamwork is needed. This was a lot to process in a rushed drive to the airport!

Home and Red Toes

Arriving at the airport in Phoenix, my incredible wife greeted me with tears in her eyes, overjoyed to have me back. She said it had been a rough week without me. That night, I washed her feet in a fun little bubble bath while she sat on the couch and we talked and caught up. Only the next day did I realize I had missed a very important detail — she had had a pedicure to surprise me, with pretty red painted toenails. Yet, I had not even noticed during the 30 minutes I spent washing and massaging her feet! Ugh! It was a funny reminder that even though we are being transformed into the image of Christ, I still had a long way to go learning how to love like Jesus!

Do not miss the red toes!
God has surprises for you.

Chapter 54

Joy Comes in the Morning (Day 40)

For His anger lasts only a moment,
but his favor lasts a lifetime;
weeping may remain for a night,
but joy comes in the morning.
PSALM 30:5

It was our Monday morning video call prayer meeting, a small group of us—former and current leaders of Christian Employee Groups at large corporations—gathering to pray. Praying with a group of believers is a powerful experience—it strengthens your relationship with God and develops your connections with them.

That morning, a friend named Kathleen, the Christian leader at a large bank, commented after hearing about my travels, *You must write a book*! We were on a video call, and I could see the determination in her eyes—I half expected her to drive over from California and force me to write it at that moment! Over the past two years, I've heard this same comment from about a dozen people, including my Iranian Muslim friend, my Jewish friend, and Jesus followers from around the world. Also, my wife and sons have also for years been encouraging me, so now I really needed to do this! During that Monday prayer meeting, I felt that God wanted me to have the first draft of the book done in just one month, by the end of November, and the full manuscript completed by the end of the year 2024. I'd never done anything like this before, but I was determined to follow

God's leading. In moments like this, I am reminded of how much I depend on the body of Christ including my family.

The Test

That evening, my wife and I attended the last Alpha Marriage class at a local church and spent the night at a nearby hotel to celebrate our 30th anniversary of being engaged. We love to celebrate all of these sorts of anniversaries! The marriage class was insightful, and we spent a lot of time talking. After being together for 30 years, you would think we would be perfectly aligned, but we are not. It became clear that night — while we deeply love and are fully committed to each other, we are not aligned in certain areas of the path God is calling me to follow. It was a difficult realization, especially in a marriage where both partners are strongly committed to Christ. That evening, God reminded me of the verses in Luke 18:29-30 and Matthew 10:37-39, which speak of following His call no matter the cost.

In my heart, I wrestled with this question: who is my first love? God? My wife? My family? My calling? God was asking me this on the eve of our 30th engagement anniversary, and I felt immense anger and frustration bubbling up.

God, really? Today? This is a day to celebrate, to be romantic!! I do not want to think about this!

I wrote in my journal that evening, feeling torn between celebration and surrender:

I feel sad. GOD, HELP! The question you ask, to choose to just follow You or not? GOD, HELP ME! Is this to teach me more faith? Do I have to reach my end? Only You can change hearts. LORD, HELP! Do I choose to follow You or my wife? God, have mercy on me!

Lord, I have vowed to You.
To go where You send me, to do what You want me to do.
I must follow You.
I surrender all to follow.
I am exhausted, no strength left.

The JOY!

Despite the internal struggle that night, the next day, our 30th engagement anniversary turned out to be one of the **best days of my life**. In my full surrender to God's plan, He blessed it. Oh, God's favor is good! I wish I could repeat that day 100 times. The blessings of my wife overwhelmed me. That dream-filled, joy-overflowing day, was God's richest gift showered on my life, and like usual, in an unexpectedly better-than-dreamed-of way.

Here's a tip for the men: spending a day at the mall shopping with your wife IS a great thing! Entering her world, getting her to try on clothes for fun, recommending items she might like, eating a snack, and just enjoying the time together — this was her love language. We both had so much fun! I had prayed that I could bless her richly on our anniversary, and that prayer was answered. It turned into the most wonderful day for us. My heart was full of joy. I wrote in my journal that evening:

*Surrender was hard. Leaving at Your feet what I love most —
my wife and family — in surrender, was heart-breaking.
Then came 100x JOY! Mark 10:30 is true! Oh God, You
challenged me to full surrender, to propel me to the edge. You
asked me to dive in, to jump, to believe, to have faith, to trust
You… it was hard… but I did it… then came JOY!
AMEN! You are always faithful!*

Mark 10:30 says,

*I tell you the truth, no one who has left home or brothers or
sisters or mother or father or children or fields for me and the
gospel will fail to receive **100 times as much** in this present
age and, in the age to come.*

God knows your situation. He will test you. As you pass the test it will unlock heaven to pour, giving you the Best Life Ever.

You want a life that is 100x more than what you have today.

Dive in, the water is great!

Chapter 55

The Choice

*you **must follow** me*
JOHN 21:22

God commands us to just follow Him.
When we follow, look at His promise! Jesus says:

*I came that they may have **LIFE**
and have it **ABUNDANTLY***
JOHN 10:10

Do you Trust God or Yourself More?

You are a follower already, of yourself or of God. God is offering His best to you, all the treasures of heaven! Does He love you? Do you trust Him? Is your plan better than His plan?

An Invitation to have the Best Life Ever

Jesus is extending His hand to you, just as He did to His first followers, asking you to *Just Follow*. Will you trust Him and take His hand? It takes courage, it will be hard, I know. God has designed you to have the best life ever! Your life and the lives of others depend on your answer. It is not just for you; it is also for the people around you that your life will bless.

Be Courageous and Third

Do you want a full, abundant life?
A life of purpose, transforming the world through love?
One that is 100 times better than what you have now?

Just Follow

Appendix A: Peek into My Prayer Life

Over the years things come and go in my time with God. For over 20 years though, I have been praying this revised *Prayer of Jabez* daily *(1 Chronicles 4:10)*. I recommend creating or using a special prayer that you pray daily. It will be an anchor in a world of change.

My morning time with God starts with...
A prayer:
   Lord, please bless me
   Please bless me indeed
   Please expand my territory
   May your hand lead me and guide me
   Please keep me from temptation,
      so that I do not cause You or anyone else pain
   Please fill me with Your joy, contentment, obedience,
      power, love and peace
   Please increase the size of my shield of faith, to deflect
      the flaming arrows of the evil one
   May I walk in courage, fearing no man
   May I never doubt my call
   Amen.

Spiritually dressing for the battle:
   I then read and pray Ephesians 6:10-20a slowly. We are in a spiritual battle daily; this reminds me of that.

A Psalm of praise and promises:
   I then slowly recite Psalm 145.

Praying for America and leadership in government:
   As I put the American flag out by our front door.

Couch time:
   Bible Reading, Journaling, Listening, and Praying... usually as I eat breakfast on the couch with a huge cup of coffee!

Appendix B: God's Love in Poetry

I do not consider myself a poet, but these thoughts and feelings came to me while finishing the book. God's merciful love has increasingly overwhelmed me these last few years.

Savor of Heaven

Soaking in love
Alone yet immersed
Brushing of arms with eternity
A tingle, a spark, a touch departed
Glimpse of radiance, glorious life
Treasures of heaven, intense glory that fills
Piercing warmth penetrates heart and soul
Eyes blink, eternity flashes, radiant light blazes
Royal heirs, myriads adorned in splendor
Fleeting brushes with glorious inheritance
Vapor fading, radiant warmth remains
Gift from the King, His treasures given
Savor of heaven

The Ruby

Glorious chamber
Once dim, coming alive
Light brightens; countless treasures radiant
Beaconing joy, love, fullness, life-filled
Space, a gap, centered for all to see
Glorious gift, on pedestal raised
Love aglow, a prize, overwhelming eyes
A jewel loaned, bequeathed to His beloved
Bursting with splendor, tasted, consumed
Enveloping and lifting, pouring and filling
Pure radiance, overflowing beauty
Red-filled ocean of love
The King's gift to me
The Ruby, my Wifey

Commentary
A bit of my internal feelings and thoughts on each of these. I have been reading St John of the Cross and his poem and commentary on *The Living Flame of Love*. The deep love and intimacy of God is something I am slowly learning. It is something rarely talked about, at least in my circles. My hope is that we, as children of God, and ultimately the bride of Christ could ponder through His passionate consuming glory-filling love of us. When we know who we are, our identity, as the treasured beloved bride of the maker of all things, God, it changes us as His love fills us.

Savor of Heaven
The *Savor of Heaven*, is how I feel God is opening my heart to the glorious beauty of being united and connected with the global Body of Christ, I feel so alive, I am becoming whole. It is a taste, a savor of heaven, getting to know my spiritual brothers and sisters now on earth, that I will be fully united with and spend all eternity with.

The Ruby
In *The Ruby* we are reminded there are many treasures God gives us, each one is a person, a member of His eternal Body. All with beautiful overwhelming fire and eternal glory. For those married, God presents us with the ultimate gift of His love for us while on earth; for me it is my jewel, my wife, *My Ruby*.
Thank you, wifey!
You are my richest treasure from God!